WHEN YOU FEEL LIKE A FAILURE

Take a Lesson from David

GENE A. GETZ

Regal
Books

A Division of GL Publications
Ventura, CA U.S.A.

ACKNOWLEDGMENT

Special thanks to Dr. Eugene Merrill, assistant professor of Semitics and Old Testament Studies at Dallas Theological Seminary, for first reading and evaluating this manuscript and offering his personal encouragement in submitting it for publication.

Other good reading by Gene A. Getz:

The Measure of a Church
The Measure of a Family
The Measure of a Man
The Measure of a Woman
The Measure of a Marriage
The Measure of a Christian—Studies in Philippians
The Measure of a Christian—Studies in Titus
The Measure of a Christian—Studies in James 1

The translation of all Regal books is under the direction of GLINT. GLINT provides technical help for the adaptation, translation and publishing of books for millions of people worldwide. For information regarding translation contact: GLINT, P.O. Box 6688, Ventura, California 93006.

Published by Regal Books
A Division of GL Publications
Ventura, California 93006
Printed in U.S.A.

Library of Congress Catalog Card No. 77-99282
ISBN 0-8307-0631-3

CONTENTS

WHY THIS STUDY?

David is well-known in history and in modern society. Christians have idealized him. Hollywood has exploited him, and artists have expertly sculptured him. And many parents are proud to name their sons "David."

But how well do we *really* know this man? What does the Bible actually say about David? And what can we learn from this man that will help us to live more devoted lives for Jesus Christ? Who was this man that God designates as "a man after His own heart" (1 Sam. 13:14)? This study will help you discover answers to these and other important questions about David.

RENEWAL—A BIBLICAL PERSPECTIVE

Renewal is the essence of dynamic Christianity and the basis on which Christians, both in a corporate or "body" sense and as individual believers, can determine the will of God. Paul made this clear when he wrote to the Roman Christians—"be transformed by the *renewing of your mind.*" Then he continued "you will be able to test and approve what God's will is" (Rom. 12:2). Here Paul is talking about renewal in a corporate sense. In other words, Paul is asking these Christians as a *body* of believers, to develop the mind of Christ through corporate renewal.

Personal renewal will not happen as God intended it unless it happens in the context of corporate renewal. On the other hand, corporate renewal will not happen as God intended without personal renewal. Both are necessary.

Biblical Renewal
Developing the mind of Christ

The larger circle represents "church renewal." This is the most comprehensive concept in the New Testament. However, every local church is made up of smaller self-contained, but interrelated units. The *family* in Scripture emerges as the "church in miniature." In turn, the family is made up of an even smaller social unit—*marriage*. The third inner circle represents *personal* renewal, which is inseparably linked to all of the other basic units. Marriage is made up of two separate individuals who become one. The family is made up of parents and children who are also to reflect the mind of Christ. And the church is made up of not only individual Christians, but couples and families.

Though all of these social units are interrelated, biblical renewal can begin within any specific social unit. But wherever it begins—in the church, families, marriages or individuals—the process immediately touches all the other social units. And one thing is certain! All that God says is consistent and harmonious. He does not have one set of principles for the church and another set for the family, another for husbands and wives and another for individual Christians. For example, the principles God outlines for local church elders, fathers and husbands regarding their role as leaders are interrelated and consistent. If they are not, we can be sure that we have not interpreted God's plan accurately.

The books listed below are part of the Biblical Renewal Series by Gene Getz designed to provide supportive help in moving toward renewal. They all fit into one of the circles described above and will provoke thought, provide interaction and tangible steps toward growth.

ONE ANOTHER SERIES	PERSONALITY SERIES	THE MEASURE OF SERIES
Building Up	Abraham	Measure of a . . .
One Another	David	Church
Encouraging	Joseph	Family
One Another	Joshua	Man
Loving	Moses	Marriage
One Another	Nehemiah	Woman
		Christian—Philippians
		Christian—Titus
		Christian—James 1

Sharpening the Focus of the Church presents an overall perspective for Church Renewal. All of these books are available from your bookstore.

A MAN AFTER GOD'S OWN HEART

1 Samuel 9:1— 16:23

Eventually David ruled as the second king of Israel. After a long and difficult process, he replaced Saul whom God rejected because of his impulsive and self-centered behavior. In fact, you cannot study the life of David without studying the life of Saul.

SAUL—A MAN AFTER HIS OWN HEART
(1 Sam. 9:1—15:35)

The story of Saul pulsates with irony. Though "there was not a more handsome person than he among the sons of Israel," he deteriorated into a weak and jealous man. Though "from his shoulders and up he was taller than any of the people," he manifested a "smallness" of character that is shocking (1 Sam. 9:2).

The story of his life is even more ironic when you study the unusual humility with which he began his career. When Samuel the prophet first approached him regarding his God-appointed post, Saul's response was sincere: "Am I not a Benjamite, of the smallest of the tribes of Israel, and my family the least of all the families of the tribe of Benjamin?" (9:21). And when his appointed time came to be king, he hid himself. The leaders of Israel had to find him and persuade him to accept the position (see 10:22,23).

Such was Saul's early attitude and behavior. But once king, he failed miserably in doing the will of God. Often he took matters into his own hands. Once he impulsively usurped the priestly office by not waiting for Samuel to arrive to offer a sacrifice to God (see 13:12). And in the space of one chapter of the Bible, 1 Samuel 15, we see Saul flagrantly disobeying God (v. 9), lying to cover up his sin (v. 13), and later rationalizing his behavior by putting the blame on others (vv. 20,21). Consequently, God rejected Saul as king (v. 28). Had he obeyed the Lord, he would have been blessed forever (see 13:13). But from this moment forward, the story of Saul is one of psychological, physical and spiritual deterioration. He became a fearful, jealous, and angry man. Dominated by his emotions, his thinking became bizarre and confused. His actions were immature and childish.

DAVID—A MAN AFTER GOD'S HEART (1 Sam. 13:14)

Saul's sin and subsequent rejection by God initiated a search for a new king. Samuel, a prophet of God, confronted Saul with a very disquieting indictment and also a staggering judgment: "But now your kingdom shall not endure. The Lord has sought out for Himself a *man after His own heart*, and the Lord has appointed him as ruler over His people, because you have not kept what the Lord commanded you" (13:14).[1]

With this sentence Saul's doom was sealed. Had he truly repented of his sins, there would have been no need for the tragic ending that characterized his final days. But his position as king of Israel was destined for years of heartache and trouble, both for Saul and Israel. David was God's heir to the throne. In God's own time, this young man would replace Saul.

THE PROCESS BEGINS (1 Sam. 16:1-13)

Though God rejected Saul as king of Israel, He still allowed him to rule for 32 years (see 13:1). But Saul did so without God's presence and power. In fact, as we'll see in the next chapter, God withdrew His Spirit from Saul and sent an evil spirit to trouble him.

The prophet Samuel, who had originally anointed Saul as king, was deeply distressed about Saul's disobedience and rejection. He was so grieved that he withdrew from his presence and "did not see Saul again until the day of his death" (15:35).

Samuel's grief is understandable. He was "old and gray" when he anointed Saul as king (12:2). He no doubt had great hopes for this brilliant and handsome young man, even though he was displeased with Israel for asking for a king (see 1 Sam. 8:6). Like an old pastor who had faithfully tended his flock, he was now ready to turn the reins of leadership over to a fresh young man, confident he would lead them forth to even greener pastures.

But such was not the case. Saul, in spite of his own great potential, and in view of God's promise to honor his rule if he obeyed Him, deliberately walked out of God's will. And, in so doing, he brought upon himself and the children of Israel the natural consequences.

There are some mistakes that can be corrected. We all fail at times. And God in His grace enables us to forget the past and move on to do even greater exploits for Him. But there are some mistakes with consequences that can never be corrected, particularly when they are made by those who are in key leadership roles. King

Saul's disobedience was his "Watergate" experience. There was no way to correct the past.

Samuel Sent by God (16:1-3)

But the work of God must go on! Disappointments in people must never thwart God's eternal purposes. And this was the Lord's message to Samuel: "How long will you grieve over Saul, since I have rejected him from being king over Israel? Fill your horn with oil, and go; I will send you to Jesse the Bethlehemite, for I have selected a king for Myself among his sons" (16:1).

Samuel's grief is revealing. He was afraid—fearful that the king would kill him if he caught Samuel searching for another leader. Saul was in open rebellion against God and against anyone who would dare to have a part in taking away his throne.

There was no doubt a second reason why Samuel was grieving. This old prophet had faithfully served as the voice of God to Israel. And it had been his responsibility to pronounce God's judgment upon Saul (see 13:14). Eventually when Saul fully realized that his doom was sealed, he turned his wrath upon Samuel, trying to kill him. Not being able to get his hands on God, he struck out at God's human mouthpiece. Samuel grieved and "did not see Saul again until the day of his death" (15:35) because he feared for his life.

Any faithful pastor and Bible teacher can identify just a little with Samuel's distress. Their God-given responsibility includes confronting others with their sins. I can personally think of incidents when I have dealt with a Christian's sins and then became the object of that person's wrath. Fortunately for most of us, our lives have never been threatened like Samuel's. But character assassination can also be very painful. This kind of grief can be difficult to bear.

But God understood Samuel's feelings just as he had

understood the fears of Abraham, Moses, and other Old Testament saints. Thus He provided a larger context—a protective, but spiritual context—in which Samuel could carry out God's purpose without being discovered by Saul. Samuel was to take a heifer to Bethlehem. There he was to offer a sacrifice to the Lord. "And you shall invite Jesse to the sacrifice," explained the Lord, "and I will show you what you shall do; and you shall anoint for Me the one whom I designate you" (16:3).

Samuel's Sacrifice to God (16:4,5)

With these specific instructions and direct encouragement from the Lord, Samuel obeyed. He "did what the Lord said, and came to Bethlehem" (16:4). The elders of the city, when they saw Samuel approaching, were very fearful. They "came trembling to meet him and said, 'Do you come in peace?'" (16:4).

Samuel was well-known in Israel as the voice of God. Often he conveyed words of judgment because of the Israelites' sin. But not this time. He had come "in peace"; he'd come "to sacrifice to the Lord" (16:5). But unknown to the people, inherent in this legitimate and sincere spiritual act of worship were two purposes: (1) the occasion of the sacrifice was a cover-up, a divine method to protect Samuel from Saul; (2) the sacrifice was the means by which Samuel would select and anoint a new king over Israel.

Samuel's Selection for God (16:6-13)

Jesse and all of his sons were invited to the sacrifice. Did this aged father know what Samuel had in mind? We can only speculate. My personal opinion is that he did. It would seem logical that Samuel and Jesse would meet for a private conference to discuss the ultimate purpose behind this rather unusual visit and sacrifice. Imagine Jesse's excitement, mingled with fatherly pride, as he prepared to parade his sons before Samuel and God. If Jesse did know about Samuel's mission we can understand why David, the youngest, was absent. Would not God choose the son with the greatest physical stature and chronological maturity? After all, Saul was the tallest man in Israel. His replacement would surely need to be someone like him in appearance.

When Jesse and his sons assembled for the sacrifice, Eliab, probably the tallest of the seven sons who were present, immediately captured Samuel's attention. "Surely the Lord's anointed is before Him," thought the old prophet (16:6).

But God had another plan, and He made it clear to Samuel: "Do not look at his appearance or at the height of his stature, because I have rejected him; for God sees not as man sees, for man looks at the outward appearance, *but the Lord looks at the heart*" (16:7).

God was looking for a man with character, a man whose heart was right toward Him. He was not interested in how tall the man was, but rather in the largeness of his soul. And as each of Jesse's sons passed before Samuel, the Lord made it clear to the old prophet that His chosen vessel was not there. Thus Samuel turned to Jesse and asked, "Are these all the children?" Jesse's response, assuming he knew the purpose of Samuel's mission, must have been one of surprise and skepticism: "There remains yet the *youngest*, and behold, he is tending the sheep" (16:11).

Samuel refused to go ahead with the sacrifice until David was invited. The moment he walked in, Samuel knew David was God's choice. Though he was a very handsome young man with red hair (he was ruddy) and soft eyes, behind this external beauty was a heart that longed to know God in deeper dimensions (see 16:12). This was a young man who, while spending long hours faithfully tending his father's sheep, one day penned some beautiful words as he led the sheep through green pastures and by still pools of fresh water, as he faithfully protected them from wild animals in secluded valleys, as he poured oil on their wounds. David saw a unique parallel between himself and God, his divine Shepherd. Inspired by both his pastoral experience and the Holy Spirit, he penned one of the most beautiful psalms ever written:

> *The Lord is my shepherd,*
> *I shall not want.*
> *He makes me lie down in green pastures;*
> *He leads me beside quiet waters.*
> *He restores my soul;*
> *He guides me in the paths of righteousness*
> *For His name's sake.*
>
> *Even though I walk through the valley of the*
> *shadow of death,*
> *I fear no evil; for Thou art with me;*
> *Thy rod and Thy staff, they comfort me;*
> *Thou dost prepare a table before me in the*
> *presence of my enemies;*
> *Thou hast anointed my head with oil;*
> *My cup overflows.*
> *Surely goodness and lovingkindness will follow*
> *me all the days of my life,*
> *And I will dwell in the house of the Lord forever.*
> Psalm 23

Here, standing before Samuel, was God's choice—a man after God's own heart. Here was the future king of Israel. Since he had been faithful in small things, God could trust him with greater things. He took good care of Jesse's sheep, and God knew He could trust him with His sheep—the children of Israel. "Arise, anoint him; for this is he," confirmed the Lord. "Then Samuel took the horn of oil and anointed him in the midst of his brothers; and the Spirit of the Lord came mightily upon David from that day forward" (1 Sam. 16:12,13).

TWENTIETH-CENTURY LESSONS

There are many lessons that emerge from this Old Testament story, but two stand out clearly.

First, we must guard our hearts against deceitful influences. Saul's life illustrates this lesson negatively. He actually began his career as a very humble and upright person. In fact the Bible states that "God changed his heart" in order to prepare him for his kingship (10:9). But prominence and success soon went to his head, which always affects the heart—the area where we are all vulnerable. Saul's old nature took over and soon dominated his total being—his attitudes and actions. Self-centeredness became a way of life.

By contrast, David illustrates this lesson positively. He was a man after *God's* heart. He desired to do the will of God, which is beautifully illustrated in Psalm 24. Wrote David:

Who may ascend into the hill of the Lord?
And who may stand in His holy place?
He who has clean hands and a pure **heart**,
Who has not lifted up his soul to falsehood,
And has not sworn deceitfully.
He shall receive a blessing from the Lord
And righteousness from the God of his salvation.
(24:3-5)

Don't misunderstand! Saul was not all bad and David all good. They were both human beings with human weaknesses. The difference lay in what dominated each man's life—self or God. They both had the same potential. But Saul more and more followed the way of self;

and David, especially in his early life when God anointed him, followed God's way very earnestly. And as we'll see later, though he sinned against God, he always repented. By contrast, Saul's efforts at repentance were superficial and, because He sees the heart, God did not respond to the king of Israel.

It's true that Saul confessed his sins (see 15:24). He wanted to be forgiven. But it's also true that his confession was based on false motives—he repented because he got caught! His position was being threatened. It was his only recourse if he wanted to maintain his kingship. David's repentance, on the other hand, always reflected godly sorrow. He had offended the God he loved. And that's a different story.

Many Christians have been sidetracked by not guarding their heart attitudes. How quickly we can go astray. Jeremiah warned against this problem when he wrote, "The *heart* is more deceitful than all else and is desperately sick" (Jer. 17:9). Solomon wrote, "Watch over your *heart* with all diligence, for from it flow the springs of life" (Prov. 4:23).

A second lesson that emerges from this story is that we must be careful when we select people for significant roles. External appearances can be very deceiving. Saul won respect because of his stature and other physical attributes. But his heart, though initially humble, was subject to deceitful influences. David also possessed many external attributes but he was a man of different internal qualities.

Today, Christians have to make many "people choices." Churches must select deacons and pastors (elders). Men who are not qualified can destroy God's work, so Paul specified very clearly in 1 Timothy 3 and Titus 1, the qualities for church leadership.

Men choose women to be their wives. And women

choose men to be their husbands. External beauty and outward appearances are not what make a marriage endure for 30 years. Yet most of us look first for these superficial attributes. In choosing a husband or wife, remember it's the heart, internal qualities, of a man or woman that reflects reality or superficiality. A mate whose heart is sensitive toward God has a heart that will be sensitive toward you.

Businessmen, too, choose associates and employees. When making any of these choices, how important it is to consider God's words to Samuel: "God sees not as man sees, for man looks at the outward appearance, but the Lord looks at the heart" (1 Sam. 16:7). Our goal in all of our people choices should be to develop God's perspective.

A FINAL WORD

Remember! Before you can put into practice the two lessons just outlined, you must have a renewed heart. And Paul in his Roman letter makes it clear how this can happen: "If you confess with your mouth, 'Jesus is Lord,' and believe in your *heart* that God raised him from the dead, you will be saved. For it is with your heart that you believe and are justified, and it is with your mouth that you confess and are saved" (Rom. 10:9,10).

Have you taken this step of faith? If you do, God will change your heart and give you new life in Christ.

Note

1. Hereafter, all italicized words and phrases in scriptural quotations are added by the author for the purpose of emphasis and clarification.

2

GOD LOOKS ON THE HEART

Psalms 8; 9; 14; 15; 19; 26; 29; 36; 37;
40; 51; 61; 65; 86; 131; 138; 139

When Samuel pronounced God's judgment on Saul, he stated that "the Lord has sought out for Himself a man after *His own heart*" (1 Sam. 13:14). In other words, Saul was *not* a man after God's heart. David was!

And later, when Samuel was looking for Saul's replacement among the sons of Jesse, God made it clear that the new king was to be chosen, not on the basis of external appearances, but on the basis of his internal qualities. "For God sees not as man sees, for man looks at the outward appearance, *but the Lord looks at the heart*" (1 Sam. 16:7).

In both the Old and New Testaments, the word "heart" refers to the center of an individual's mental, emotional and spiritual life. Put another way, the heart is the "innermost part of man." The heart reflects the real person. As the *mental* center, the heart knows,

16

understands, reflects, considers and remembers. As the *emotional* center, it is the seat of joy, courage, pain, anxiety, despair, sorrow and fear. As the *moral* center God "tries the heart," "sees the heart." "refines the heart" and "searches the heart." The Scriptures make it clear that a person may have an "evil heart," be "godless in heart," be "perverse and deceitful in heart" and he can "harden his heart." However, a person may also have a "clean heart" and a "new heart."[1]

To understand David as a person there are two basic questions that need to be asked and answered. If he was a man after God's heart, then *what was David's view of God?* If God selected him, not on the basis of his external person, but on the basis of his heart, then *what was God's view of David?* The psalms give us a unique and rich source to answer these questions. Most scholars believe that David wrote at least 73 of these poetic expressions. And what he wrote communicates clearly David's view of God and God's view of David.[2]

WHAT WAS DAVID'S VIEW OF GOD?
(Pss. 19; 29; 65; 139; 8; 36)

Practically every psalm David penned gives us insight into his ideas, attitudes and feelings toward God. Consequently we can only highlight the answer for this first question.

The Omnipotent Creator

Several of David's psalms focus extensively on God's creative power. David was an outdoorsman, a man who spent many hours, day and night, absorbing the splendor, beauty and mysteries of nature. At times, inspired by God's Spirit, he put his thoughts on paper. Such is Psalm 19, which expresses David's convictions and feelings about the firmament, and particularly the sun in its journey across space:

The heavens are telling of the glory of God;
And the firmament is declaring the work
   of His hands.
Day to day pours forth speech,
And night to night reveals knowledge.
There is no speech, nor are there words;
Their voice is not heard.
Their line has gone out through all the earth,
And their utterances to the end of the world.
In them He has placed a tent for the sun,
Which is as a bridegroom coming out
   of his chamber;
It rejoices as a strong man to run his course.
Its rising is from one end of the heavens,
And its circuit to the other end of them;
And there is nothing hidden from its heat.
(19:1-6)

David's view of God's creative power in nature often
generated praise, thanksgiving and worship in his heart.
How clearly this can be seen in Psalm 29 as he wrote
about a storm. While most of us focus on our fears and
anxieties in the midst of this kind of natural turbulence,
David's heart focused on God. To him the phenomenon
he observed, heard and felt reflected the voice of the
Lord:

The voice of the Lord is upon the waters;
The God of glory thunders,
The Lord is over many waters.
The voice of the Lord is powerful,
The voice of the Lord is majestic.
The voice of the Lord breaks the cedars;
Yes, the Lord breaks in pieces
   the cedars of Lebanon.
And He makes Lebanon skip like a calf,
And Sirion like a young wild ox.

The voice of the Lord hews out flames of fire.
The voice of the Lord shakes the wilderness;
The Lord shakes the wilderness of Kadesh.
The voice of the Lord makes the deer to calve,
And strips the forests bare,
And in His temple everything says, "Glory!"
(29:3-9)

Another facet of God's power in nature that impressed David involved the seasons, and God's provisions to cause the earth to produce all kinds of vegetation, which in turn provided sustenance for both mankind and animals. This is clearly expressed in a portion of Psalm 65:

Thou dost visit the earth, and cause it to
overflow;
Thou dost greatly enrich it;
The stream of God is full of water;
Thou dost prepare their grain, for thus Thou
dost prepare the earth.
Thou dost water its furrows abundantly;
Thou dost settle its ridges;
Thou dost soften it with showers;
Thou dost bless its growth.
Thou hast crowned the year with Thy bounty,
And Thy paths drip with fatness.
The pastures of the wilderness drip,
And the hills gird themselves with rejoicing.
The meadows are clothed with flocks,
And the valleys are covered with grain;
They shout for joy, yes, they sing.
(65:9-13)

The Omniscient God

David also viewed God as *all-knowing.* He recognized that God knew everything about him—every de-

tail of his heart and his actions—at any given moment.
Note the opening verses of Psalm 139:

> *O Lord, Thou hast searched me and known me.*
> *Thou dost know when I sit down and when I rise up;*
> *Thou dost understand my thought from afar.*
> *Thou dost scrutinize my path and my lying down,*
> *And art intimately acquainted with all my ways.*
> *Even before there is a word on my tongue,*
> *Behold, O Lord, Thou dost know it all.*
> *Thou hast enclosed me behind and before,*
> *And laid Thy hand upon me.*
> *Such knowledge is too wonderful for me;*
> *It is too high, I cannot attain to it.*
> (139:1-6)

The Omnipresent Spirit

David not only viewed God as omnipotent and omniscient, but also as present everywhere. In other words,
there was no place David could go but that God was
there to guide, to protect, to comfort and to search out
his heart:

> *Where can I go from Thy Spirit?*
> *Or where can I flee from Thy presence?*
> *If I ascend to heaven, Thou art there;*
> *If I make my bed in Sheol, behold, Thou art*
>   *there.*
> *If I take the wings of the dawn,*
> *If I dwell in the remotest part of the sea,*
> *Even there Thy hand will lead me,*
> *And Thy right hand will lay hold of me.*
> *If I say, "Surely the darkness will overwhelm me,*
> *And the light around me will be night,"*
> *Even the darkness is not dark to Thee,*
> *And the night is as bright as the day.*
> *Darkness and light are alike to Thee.*
> (139:7-12)

The God of Loving Concern

Seeing God's power in nature led David to appreciate more fully God's loving concern for mankind. The fact that the Lord gave human beings a certain degree of authority and control over His natural creation overwhelmed David. This is expressed in Psalm 8:

When I consider Thy heavens,
*   the work of Thy fingers,*
The moon and the stars, which Thou hast ordained;
What is man, that Thou dost take thought of him?
And the son of man, that Thou dost care for him?
Yet Thou hast made him a little lower than God,
And dost crown him with glory and majesty!
Thou dost make him to rule over the works
*   of Thy hands;*
Thou hast put all things under his feet,
All sheep and oxen,
And also the beasts of the field,
The birds of the heavens, and the fish of the sea,
Whatever passes through the paths of the seas.

O Lord, our Lord,
How majestic is Thy name in all the earth!
(8:3-9)

The God of Lovingkindness, Faithfulness and Righteousness

The vastness of the universe also reminded David of God's *personal* attributes. Thus he wrote in Psalm 36:

Thy lovingkindness, O Lord,
*   extends to the heavens,*
Thy faithfulness reaches to the skies.
Thy righteousness is like the mountains of God;
Thy judgments are like a great deep.
(36:5,6)

There are, of course, many other psalms that reveal *David's view of God.* But these few we have read demonstrate dramatically why David was "a man after God's heart."

WHAT WAS GOD'S VIEW OF DAVID?
(Pss. 9; 86; 138; 15; 26; 139; 37; 40; 19; 51; 131; 61)

We've looked at David's view of God. But how did God view David? When the Lord looked beyond this young man's outward appearance and looked at his heart, what did He see? Again, the psalms give us a significant profile on David's inner qualities.

A Believing Heart

When God looked at David's heart He saw a heart that believed in His existence. So convinced was David of this existence that He wrote: "The *fool* has said in his *heart*, 'There is no God' " (Ps. 14:1; 53:1). One thing is clear. When God looked at David's heart the day he was chosen to be king, He saw a heart that believed in His existence. To David, any man who denied the existence of God was a fool.

A Thankful Heart

God also saw a thankful heart—a heart that was totally overwhelmed with God's love and provisions. This is reflected in a number of psalms David wrote.

I will give thanks to the Lord with all my **heart;**
I will tell of all Thy wonders.
I will be glad and exult in Thee;
I will sing praise to Thy name, O Most High.
(9:1,2)

Teach me Thy way, O Lord;
I will walk in Thy truth;
Unite my **heart** *to fear Thy name.*

22

I will give thanks to Thee, O Lord my God,
    with all my **heart,**
And will glorify Thy name forever.
(86:11,12)

I will give Thee thanks with all my **heart;**
I will sing praises to Thee before the gods.
I will bow down toward Thy holy temple,
And give thanks to Thy name
    for Thy lovingkindness and Thy truth;
For Thou hast magnified Thy word according
    to all Thy name.
(138:1,2)

A Truthful Heart

David's view of God caused him to want to reflect God's character. This is obvious in Psalm 15:
O Lord, who may abide in Thy tent?
Who may dwell on Thy holy hill?
He who walks with integrity,
    and works righteousness,
And speaks truth in his **heart.**
He does not slander with his tongue,
Nor does evil to his neighbor,
Nor takes up a reproach against his friend.
(15:1-3)

An Open Heart

David knew God was omniscient. He did not try to hide from God. His heart was open and transparent.
Examine me, O Lord, and try me;
Test my mind and my **heart.**
(26:2)

Search me, O God, and know my **heart;**
Try me and know my anxious thoughts;

And see if there be any hurtful way in me,
And lead me in the everlasting way.
(139:23,24)

An Expectant Heart

David trusted God to meet his needs.
Delight yourself in the Lord;
And He will give you the desires of your **heart.**
Commit your way to the Lord,
Trust also in Him and He will do it.
(37:4,5)

A Heart that Remembered God's Law

Because David wanted to do God's will in all things, he committed the law of God to memory. Thus he could write: "I delight to do Thy will, O my God; Thy Law is *within my heart*" (40:8).

And in Psalm 19 David explained even more graphically his attitude toward God's Word:
The judgments of the Lord are true; they are
righteous altogether.
They are more desirable than gold, yes, than
much fine gold;
Sweeter also than honey and the drippings of
the honeycomb.
Moreover, by them Thy servant is warned;
In keeping them there is great reward.
(19:9-11)

And then David culminated his concern about doing the will of God with this prayer:
Let the words of my mouth and the meditation
of my **heart**
Be acceptable in Thy sight,
O Lord, my rock and my redeemer.
(19:14)

A Repentant Heart

When David sinned against God, he demonstrated a truly repentant heart. Unlike Saul, who sought forgiveness because he had been caught and was in danger of losing his position, David sought forgiveness because he had failed the God he loved. Thus, in Psalm 51, he prayed:

Create in me a clean **heart**, *O God,*
And renew a steadfast spirit within me.

And later with confidence he prayed yet further:

The sacrifices of God are a broken spirit;
A broken *and a contrite* **heart**, *O God, Thou wilt not despise.*

(51:10,17)

A Humble Heart

David knew his limitations. His view of himself was commensurate with God's greatness. He knew he had strengths but he also knew he had weaknesses.

When God looked upon David's heart He saw a man with a proper balance in the area of self-image. This is reflected in one of David's shortest psalms:

O Lord, my **heart** *is not proud, or my eyes haughty;*
Nor do I involve myself in great matters,
Or in things too difficult for me.

(131:1)

A Dependent Heart

David knew how much he needed God to sustain him. He could not fulfill his responsibilities in his own strength. Note his prayer in Psalm 61:

Hear my cry, O God;
Give heed to my prayer.
From the end of the earth I call to Thee, when my **heart** *is faint;*
Lead me to the rock that is higher than I.

For Thou hast been a refuge for me,
A tower of strength against the enemy.
Let me dwell in Thy tent forever;
Let me take refuge in the shelter of Thy wings.
(61:1-4)

When God looked at David that day he was anointed king, He saw a man after His own heart—a man who understood who God really is. For David was deeply affected by the reality of God's omnipotence, His omniscience, His omnipresence, His lovingkindness, faithfulness and righteousness.

But God also saw a man who was personally affected by his perceptions of the Lord of the universe. And looking beyond David's attractive red hair, beautiful eyes and handsome appearance, the Lord saw a man with a believing heart, a thankful heart, a truthful heart, an open heart, an expectant heart, a heart that cherished God's law, a repentant heart and a humble and dependent heart. This is why God chose David to be the future king of Israel.

TWENTIETH-CENTURY LESSONS

David was not a perfect man. But he had a proper view of God, which affected his own heart and caused him to be a person God could use, in spite of his human weaknesses. What about you? What is your view of God? And what is His view of you? When you think about God, what goes through your mind and your emotions? When God looks beyond your external appearance, what does He see?

David's view of God should be our view of God. The following questions will help you evaluate your view of God:

1. When I think of God's *omnipotence* (that He is

all-powerful) how does it affect my life? How could it affect my life?

2. When I think of God's *omniscience* (that He knows everything) how does it affect my life? How could it affect my life?

3. When I think of God's *omnipresence* (that He is present everywhere) how does it affect my life? How could it affect my life?

4. When I think of God's *loving concern* for all men (and for me personally) how does it affect my life? How could it affect my life?

5. When I think of God's *faithfulness* how does it affect my life? How could it affect my life?

6. When I think of God's *righteousness*, His *holiness*, how does it affect my life? How could it affect my life?

God's view of David should be His view of us. Using David's example, evaluate your own heart attitudes. On the following check list rate your personal evaluation: 1=never; 2=sometimes; 3=much of the time; 4=all of the time

☐ 1. I have a believing heart
☐ 2. I have a thankful heart
☐ 3. I have a truthful heart
☐ 4. I have an open heart
☐ 5. I have an expectant heart
☐ 6. I have a repentant heart
☐ 7. I have a humble heart
☐ 8. I have a dependent heart
☐ 9. I am regularly filling my heart with the Word of God.

Pinpoint the areas of your life where you need the most improvement in your view of God and in God's view of you. Determine that, with God's help, you will become more and more conformed to His will.

27

WARNING!! Don't be discouraged. God is in the business of changing human hearts. REMEMBER!! He *is* the omnipotent, omniscient, and omnipresent God. If He can control the universe, He can control your life— *if* you'll let Him. The process, however, must begin with you, your will, your desire to have Him change you. God will not force Himself on you.

Notes

1. For a list of Scriptures to verify the functions of the heart, see Charles F. Pfeiffer et al., eds., *Wycliffe Bible Encyclopedia*, (Chicago: Moody Press, 1975), vol. 1, pp. 767, 768.

2. There is no absolute way to prove the Davidic authorship of most of these psalms. The notations in most versions of the Bible that attribute certain of these psalms to David are not a part of the original and inspired text. However, it is commonly accepted that in the most part, these are accurate notations and these 73 psalms are traditionally attributed to David.

3

AN AWESOME CONTRAST

1 Samuel 16:1-23

When David stepped forth to be anointed the second king of Israel, the Bible records for us a very awesome and sharp contrast. First, we read that "the Spirit of the Lord *came mightily upon David*" (16:13). This is followed immediately by an opposite statement that is startling: "Now the Spirit of the Lord *departed from Saul*" (1 Sam. 16:14).

ANOINTING OF THE HOLY SPIRIT

In the Old Testament we frequently read that the Spirit of God came upon men whom God sovereignly selected for special tasks, especially that they might prophesy and speak God's Word to the children of Israel. For example, the Lord selected Bezalel to help build the Tabernacle in the wilderness and anointed him in a special way by His Spirit. The Lord told Moses, "I have *filled him with the Spirit of God* in wisdom, in understanding, in knowledge, and in all kinds of craftsmanship, to make artistic designs for work in gold, in silver, and in bronze, and in the cutting of stones for settings, and in the carving of wood, that he may work in all kinds of craftsmanship" (Exod. 31: 3-5). This is an Old Testament example of "spiritual gifts" that God sovereignly gave to certain men in Israel to achieve His divine purposes.

Moses, of course, was also a recipient of God's special anointing. But at one time in his life when he was terribly discouraged with what appeared to be an impossible task, namely successfully leading the children of Israel through the wilderness and into the Promised Land, God anointed a number of other men to help him. "The Lord therefore said to Moses, 'Gather for Me seventy men from the elders of Israel, whom you know to be the elders of the people and their officers and bring them to the tent of meeting, and let them take their stand there with you. Then I will come down and speak with you there, and *I will take of the Spirit who is upon you, and will put Him upon them;* and they shall bear the burden of the people with you, so that you shall not bear it all alone' " (Num. 11:16,17).[1]

Other illustrations of this Old Testament phenomenon included Balaam (see Num. 24:2), Joshua (see Num. 27:18; Deut. 34:9), Othniel (see Judg. 3:10), Gideon (see Judg. 6:34), Jephthah (see Judg. 11:29), and most of those who were called judges in Israel. We all remember Samson who was given special strength by the Spirit to achieve unusual feats of valor (see Judg. 14:6,19; 15:14). With all of these men the Spirit of the Lord *came upon them*, giving them supernatural abilities.[2] God also did this for Saul when he was chosen to be the first king of Israel. We read that "God changed his heart. . . . and the *Spirit of God came upon him mightily*" (1 Sam. 10:9,10), just as He did on David the day he was also anointed to be Saul's replacement.

THE HOLY SPIRIT DEPARTED FROM SAUL
(1 Sam. 16:1-15)

Saul's life unfolds tragically and in dramatic proportions, however, when the Spirit came upon David but *departed* from Saul. This contrast is significant. Seldom do we read in the Old Testament that God, after anointing a person in a special way with His Spirit, deliberately withdrew His Spirit. It *is* true that the influence of His Spirit in certain gifted men was more obvious at certain times, such as in Samson's life. But in between these unusual manifestations, the Spirit evidently did not depart from these men as He did from Saul, even when they were living carnal lives.[3] Later David was afraid that he might lose the Spirit because of his horrendous sins (he no doubt remembered vividly what had happened to Saul). Thus he prayed that the Lord would not take His Holy Spirit from him (see Ps. 51:11). But because of David's sincere repentance, which is reflected in the total context of Psalm 51, it evidently never happened.

But Saul did lose the Holy Spirit! And the reason was his persistent disobedience and his heart attitude. When confronted by Samuel, Saul defended his behavior with rationalizations and dishonest excuses. And when he discovered he could not manipulate the Lord, his heart became even more hardened.

There appears to be another factor in explaining God's actions toward Saul: to whom God gives much, He expects much. Jesus stated this principle very clearly in one of His parables (see Luke 12:42-48). And Saul *had* been given much. God's Spirit was mightily upon him. And in the full light of God's special grace he disobeyed the Lord and was unwilling to sincerely acknowledge his sin. Rather he hardened his heart.

GOING FROM BAD TO WORSE

Unfortunately a step backward in rebellion toward God often leads to another. Once the "Spirit of the Lord departed from Saul . . . an evil spirit from the Lord terrorized him" (1 Sam. 16:14).

This very unusual event in Old Testament history needs some careful explanation and elaboration. What actually happened to make this awesome contrast we've been talking about even more awesome? There are two main opinions among Bible scholars.

An Evil Spirit

First, some believe that this was indeed an evil spirit. Though Saul's symptoms reflected what might be interpreted as psychological disturbance, they conclude that the direct cause of that disturbance was an outside force that had access to his inner being. Though he suffered great periods of neurotic anxiety and emotional stress, alternating between deep depression and fits of rage, they believe the root cause was directly demonic—not merely psychological.

If this interpretation is correct, once God's Spirit departed from him, Saul may have engaged in occult practices that were very prevalent in the pagan world. Having keenly sensed that his supernatural abilities from God had been taken away, it would be only natural for a man like Saul in his insecurity and anger to reach out to whatever source he could to regain them. And Satan and his cohorts represent, then as now, a powerful and evil source that is nearer to every one of us than we often realize. The apostle Paul was well aware of this reality when he told the Ephesian Christians that their struggle was "not against flesh and blood, but against the rulers, against the authorities, against the powers of this dark world and against the spiritual forces of evil in the heavenly realms" (Eph. 6:12). King Saul may have turned to these "forces of evil" once the Lord's Spirit left him.

If the evil spirit troubling Saul was indeed a demon, how do we explain that this evil personage came "from the Lord"? This would probably refer to the fact that God *permitted* the spirit to come upon Saul. It would be a reference to the Lord's sovereign control over all things. Though He has given Satan and his company of evil spirits a great deal of freedom, they cannot do anything without God's permission, especially in the lives of His children (see Job 1—2). And Saul, without doubt, was one of God's true children. Disobedient, yes! But a child of God nevertheless. But as a free moral agent, he had the liberty to turn away from God and to dabble in this world of evil. But, if he did, with that step came terrible consequences. He was caught in the clutches of an evil spirit.

I can accept this interpretation as valid, especially since Saul in his final days participated in a seance (see 1 Sam. 28:7), but there is yet another opinion that seems more feasible.

A Psychological Condition

The word "evil" can legitimately refer to discontent, calamity, or disaster. Thus the Lord could have sent to Saul this kind of "spirit" or sense of distress and anxiety. Rather than being an outside evil force, sent as a demon, the "spirit" could have been a psychological condition within Saul's inner being, resulting directly from God's judgment upon him. Therefore, Saul's case would be different from demon possession and also different from a typical psychological problem. The manifestation

33

could be quite similar but the cause would be from another source.

Whatever the interpretation, one thing needs to be made clear. Without doubt Saul brought this condition on himself. It began with Saul's outright disobedience to God's personal and direct communication with him. And once God's Spirit left him, Saul deteriorated in his relationship both with God and people. Though Saul could have thrown himself upon God's mercy to deliver him from his uncomfortable and difficult state, he chose to try to solve the problem in his own strength. But even then we see God continuing to reach out to Saul in love. In fact, God's judgment was discipline—an act of love designed to turn Saul's heart back toward righteousness.

GOD'S GRACE TOWARD SAUL (1 Sam. 16:16-23)

Much of the story of David's life is in reality the story of God's grace toward Saul. In some respects Saul represents the Christian in rebellion against God, and David reflects God's love through Jesus Christ.

Saul's servants immediately recognized Saul's problem; thus they suggested to Saul that they find someone who could play quiet and melodic music, specifically music from a harp (see 16:16).

Saul's response to this suggestion was positive (see 16:17). And just by *chance*, one of Saul's servants had become acquainted with David. Just by *chance* he knew that David was a "skillful musician, a mighty man of valor, a warrior, one prudent in speech, and a handsome man." The servant also knew that the Lord was with David (see 16:18).

From the perspective of history, it is very clear that these events were not "by chance." Rather, David, the man who was going to eventually replace Saul, provided the means whereby Saul could find relief from the spirit that was troubling him. Also Saul would have opportunity to learn firsthand from David what kind of man God honors. Since Saul would not listen to Samuel, God, in this grace, exposed him to David.

From this passage we see that David had instant rapport with the king of Israel. Saul "loved him greatly" (16:21). David not only served the king in his court, soothing his troubled spirit with God's Word set to music (also a reflection of God's grace toward Saul), but he also became his armor-bearer. This "man after God's own heart" was constantly in Saul's presence.

God's grace toward Saul is also evident in that He gave Saul many more years to learn these lessons. Though He had rejected him as king, He did not immediately dethrone him. And God in no way rejected him as His child. It is in direct keeping with God's nature that David *could* have become Saul's deliverer and saviour had Saul humbled himself before God and truly repented. Those years of transition from the time Saul was rejected until David became king could have been Saul's happiest and most productive. As it turned out they were his most miserable and disastrous, primarily because he continued to reject God's love and grace.

A NEW TESTAMENT PERSPECTIVE

This incident, concerning Saul's disobedience and the results of it, raises several questions in the minds of Christians.

Will the Holy Spirit Ever Leave a Christian?

When studying the ministry of the Holy Spirit in the Old Testament, it is imperative that Christians understand the viewpoint of the New Testament. Though it is true that the Holy Spirit also came upon certain individuals in New Testament days in unusual ways, particularly upon the apostles, and gave them special power and revelations from God which were very similar to Old Testament events, it is also true that He came to indwell *every* person who was truly converted to Jesus Christ. Thus Paul wrote: "For we were *all* baptized by one Spirit into one body" (1 Cor. 12:13). And Peter proclaimed for all to hear in Jerusalem that the promise of the Spirit is for *all* people who respond to the gospel (see Acts 2:39).

In the Old Testament God gave His Spirit only to certain people whom He chose to serve as His prophets and special leaders. And as we've seen in Saul's case, under certain circumstances the Lord's Spirit departed from men. But not so in the New Testament. Jesus said to His followers, "I will ask the Father, and he will give you another Counselor, the Spirit of truth, *to be with you forever.* The world cannot accept this Counselor, because it neither sees him nor knows him. But you know him, for he lives with you and *will be in you*" (John 14:16,17).

In summary then, there are at least three unique differences between the Old Testament and the New Testament in relationship to the Holy Spirit. In the New Testament the indwelling presence of the Spirit related to *becoming* God's children—conversion to Jesus Christ. In the Old Testament it follows then that the Spirit indwelled only certain select believers; in the New Testament He indwelled *all* believers. In the Old Testament, under certain circumstances God would remove His Holy Spirit from an individual; in the New Testament God has promised that His Spirit would never leave. And we can rest in the security of God's promises. He cannot lie.

What About Demon Possession?

There are many illustrations of demon possession in the New Testament. The Gospel records are filled with accounts where Jesus encountered demon-possessed people and healed them. And while Christ was still on earth and after He ascended to heaven, the apostles and other select Christians were given the same power to cast out demons. Paul certainly encountered these problems in his ministry.

Is There Such a Thing as Demon Possession Today?

I believe there is demon possession today, but I also believe that much that is attributed to demons are reflections of spiritual and psychological problems. Though the problems may be the direct result of sin, they are not caused by direct contact with Satan or evil spirits.

I've counseled a number of people over the years with very severe problems. In all of these cases I doubt very much if I've ever seen an authentic case of demon possession (maybe one). But I must acknowledge that my counseling has been limited to people (both Christians and non-Christians) who have been directly influenced by the message of Christianity. Whether historians, sociologists and anthropologists acknowledge it or not, the American culture has been deeply affected by both Old and New Testament precepts and ideas.

Many missionaries, however, who have ministered outside of the Western culture, have encountered people who are totally pagan in their religion and lifestyle. Many of these servants of the Lord are thoroughly convinced that they have observed bona fide demon possession. And though I believe some of the cases they've encountered are also rooted in psychological disturbance, I am convinced that many of the cases are real and very similar to the types of problems Jesus encountered when He walked the face of the earth.

But it is true that, as Americans, we have seen an increase in demonic activity in recent years in the

United States, particularly due to the drug culture. People have opened their minds and hearts to the world of the occult and some people actually worship Satan. Under these circumstances, there is no question that demon possession can become a reality.

Can a Christian Ever Become Demon Possessed?

There is a difference of opinion among well-informed Christian scholars regarding the answer to this question. Some give a decided yes; others give a decided no. And some Christians believe that a Christian can be harassed or *oppressed* by an evil spirit, but never *possessed*. The problem with this is that we have no real way to define these concepts biblically.

Personally, I do not believe this question can be resolved only by the study of Scripture. But I tend to believe (and this is an opinion) that demon possession can happen to a Christian if he willfully turns his back on God and dabbles in the occult—perhaps as Saul did.

On the other hand it's very clear in Scripture that Satan and his evil forces cannot touch a Christian who resists his approaches. James wrote: "Submit yourselves, then, to God. *Resist the devil, and he will flee from you.* Come near to God and he will come near to you" (Jas. 4:7,8). And Paul wrote: "Put on the full armor of God so that you can take your stand against the devil's schemes" (Eph. 6:11). In Christ we have all the protection we need.

TWENTIETH-CENTURY LESSONS

What are some lessons we can learn from Saul's awesome experience?

Develop a correct view of God. On the one hand God is not out to punish Christians when they disobey Him. Rather He disciplines in a patient, loving and kind way.

He has already forgiven us in Jesus Christ. His desire is that we now walk in His ways and do His will. If we are true believers, He will never take His Holy Spirit from us. His grace continues to reach out to people, long after they have totally rejected Him.

On the other hand, don't take God's love and grace for granted. The Bible says there comes a time when He gives people up to go their own way. In this sense we can determine our own course and we will suffer the natural consequences (see Rom. 1:24-32). And even among Christians there will be those who are saved, as Paul says, "only as one escaping through the flames" (1 Cor. 3:15). Personally I do not want to stand before God under these circumstances. I want to have loved Christ as He loved me—as much as that is possible on this earth.

Never dabble in the occult. Christians should beware of the occult, including Ouija boards and astrology. Further, be extremely cautious about ESP experiments. Some of these activities may appear harmless but they may also be very dangerous, especially for people who are impressionable and/or psychologically distressed.

"Let us fix our eyes on Jesus, the Pioneer and Perfecter of our faith" (Heb. 12:2). Let us resist Satan knowing he will flee from us. Let us "stand firm then, with the belt of truth . . . , with the breastplate of righteousness . . . , and with [our] feet fitted with the gospel of peace." Also let us "take up the shield of faith . . . [and] the helmet of salvation and the sword of the Spirit, which is the word of God." And finally we should "pray in the Spirit on all occasions" (Eph. 6:14-18).

Don't confuse psychological problems with demon activity. As a general rule, particularly among people who have had no direct contact with the occult, persistent problems of anxiety, obsessions, compulsions, depression and anger are rooted in personal problems that are psychological and spiritual in nature. To attribute these problems to Satan's direct influence can only make them worse. And furthermore, to attribute these to God's judgment can also be devastating to an already emotionally disturbed person. It seems Saul's case was unique, no matter what the interpretation regarding the cause of his problem; it *was* because of God's judgment. But this does not represent the normal state of things when people have psychological difficulties.

I frequently talk with people who have been plagued with obsessions, that is, thoughts that continually intrude into their minds. Some of these people have attributed these obsessions to Satan—or to the Holy Spirit. Interestingly, however, the more they resist the obsession, the more it dominates them. This is a sure sign of a psychological obsession. The more you resist it, the more it controls you.

If these obsessions are from Satan, according to the Scriptures, as we resist them Satan will leave us alone. He will flee from us. If the thoughts are from the Holy Spirit, He will certainly help us rather than make the problem worse.

Let me give you a specific case in point. I counseled with a very sincere Christian man who was periodically obsessed with the thought that he did not love his wife. It was obvious to me that he *did* love his wife, but somehow he could not get the negative thought out of his mind when it attacked him. My advice to him was not to resist the thought but to accept it as a psychological obsession that was not based in fact. I also reassured him that I knew that he loved his wife and gave him factual evidence for my observation. Consequently, by taking this advice he was able to dissipate the obsession. However, the more he would fight the problem in his mind, the more strongly it controlled him. It's obvious from this illustration that the obsession had nothing to do with either the Holy Spirit or an evil spirit. It was rooted in his psychological nature.

There are many and complex reasons why people experience obsessions. Part of the cause goes back to guilt problems in childhood. A very sensitive person who has repressed his feelings of guilt and anxiety often will have obsessions. Obviously you cannot help a person overcome this kind of problem by attributing the obsession to Satan or even to the Holy Spirit.

Let me give you one other illustration that helps to clarify why it is so vital to differentiate between problems that are rooted in the psychological and those that may be caused by a direct influence of Satan. One evening, following a church service, I encountered a young man who was extremely disturbed. He was in great emotional agony and asked that I pray for him. He told me he felt that he was possessed by a demon.

There were several other pastors who were present at this time and I asked them to join me in prayer for this young man. One of the pastors volunteered to take charge of the situation, indicating that he had had previous experience casting out demons.

I willingly turned the problem over to him and simply observed the process. After approximately an hour of what was supposed to be an exorcism, the young man was getting worse. His frustration was increasing and the contortions of his body and speech were very noticeable. During this process, however, I made a number of observations that had distinct psychological overtones. I asked if I might not talk to the boy. I knelt down beside him and began to interpret his problem psychologically on the basis of the data I had put together in my mind watching the process. His reactions were immediate and, in fact, he appeared shocked at my insight. "Is God telling you what I'm thinking?" he asked in a startled manner. "No" I said, "I'm simply interpreting your problem psychologically."

From that moment on the boy relaxed. When he had gained control of himself I asked him why he had gone through the contortions he had. His answer was more startling than his quick recovery. He told us he did not want to disappoint us. If we thought he had a demon he wanted to conform to our expectations. He also went on to relate the fact that he had heard an evangelist talk about casting out demons. Further, this speaker had described very vividly how demons control people. It was obvious that this impressionable young man had identified his inner psychological struggles with what the evangelist had described as demon possession and was attempting to sincerely simulate the situation.

Don't get me wrong. He was not being dishonest. He actually was trying to get at the root of his problem. And he really believed he was demon possessed. The fact of the matter is that he was psychologically disturbed, primarily because of extensive guilt over past and present behavior. And the meeting he had been in accentuated his guilt so severely that he actually felt he was being attacked by a demon.

The conclusion is obvious. Had we left this young man in a state of turmoil, believing he had a demon that could not be cast out, it's no telling what may have happened to him. This illustration left an indelible impression on my mind as to how important it is to differentiate between problems that are psychological and spiritual in origin from those that are not. It is dangerous to dabble in demonism, including attempting to exorcise or contact them.

A FINAL WORD

Whatever a Christian's problem, there are two verses

of Scripture that stand firm as foundation stones and can provide a believer with fantastic security. They are Paul's words to the Romans: "For I am convinced that neither death nor life, neither angels *nor demons*, [including evil forces], neither height nor depth, *nor anything else in all creation* [including Satan], will be able to separate us from the love of God that is in Christ Jesus our Lord" (Rom. 8:38,39).

Notes

1. Note that in this case Moses was directed by the Lord to select the men and God anointed them with the Spirit. Ordinarily God Himself made the selection.

2. A number of others in Israel, whom the Lord called prophets, also had direct contact with God by His Spirit. Many are named and became authors of Old Testament books, but many are identified only as a part of a group, such as in 1 Samuel 10:5,6.

3. There's an interesting correlation between believers who were especially gifted by the Spirit in the Old Testament and those who were especially gifted by the Spirit in the New Testament. For example, the Corinthians were the most spiritually gifted church, yet they were the most carnal church. But their carnality did not cause God to take away their special gifts. God even allowed them to use the gifts to promote their own selfish ambitions.

4

THE BATTLE IS THE LORD'S

1 Samuel 17:1-58

The story of David and Goliath represents one of the most dramatic events in the history of Israel. Before David met Goliath he was little known, even though he had served as Saul's personal musician and one of his armor-bearers. After David encountered this powerful Philistine warrior and won a decisive victory, he not only became a popular figure in Israel but also became well-known among the nations that surrounded God's chosen people. All of this, of course, was within God's plan and purpose for David. God provided him with a unique opportunity to prove himself and David responded.

THE STORY IN PERSPECTIVE (1 Sam. 17:1-58)

On an earlier occasion God had granted Israel a miraculous victory over the Philistine army. By all human standards, Israel should have been defeated mercilessly. However, the Lord's blessing was still upon Saul and consequently upon Israel. Even though they were ill equipped for war, God assisted Israel with an earthquake, creating terrible confusion in the Philistine camp (see 14:12-23). Consequently, Israel won an unusual victory.

But in their own hearts the Philistines were not to be denied. They desperately wanted to capture Israel and bring them under their dominion. They regrouped and once again "gathered their armies for battle." This time, however, their tactic was different. Because of their severe defeat and loss of life at Michmash, they decided to confront Israel with a single warrior who would challenge a representative from Israel. As was common in warfare in those days, the battle would be won or lost without sacrificing numerous lives. The side that won through the representative would voluntarily become servants of the other.

The Philistine Warrior

The Philistine representative was a sight to behold. He stood at least nine feet six inches tall. Even Saul, who from the shoulders up was taller than any other man in Israel, would appear as a dwarf compared with Goliath.

Every day, twice a day, for 40 days—the huge Philistine descended to the valley floor and shouted up to the children of Israel, challenging someone to come out and fight him. His words were clear and crisp and very foreboding to Israel: "Why do you come out to draw up in battle array? Am I not the Philistine and you servants of Saul? Choose a man for yourselves and let him come down to me. If he is able to fight with me and kill me, then we will become your servants; but if I prevail against him and kill him, then you shall become our servants and serve us" (17:8,9).

The results were devastating. "When Saul and all Israel heard these words of the Philistine, they were dismayed and greatly afraid" (17:11). There wasn't a man in the army of Israel who dared to accept the challenge. Especially since their leader, the tallest of them all, was paralyzed with fear.

Israel's Representative

But then it happened! The unexpected! David had been fulfilling two jobs, playing his harp for Saul during his periods of depression and in between times helping his father. When Goliath first appeared, David was back home tending his father Jesse's sheep. However, some time during the 40 days when Goliath was shouting out his challenge, Jesse asked David to take some food to his three older brothers who were serving in Saul's army and to also see how they were faring.

When David arrived on the scene, he saw Goliath descend the mountain and heard him shout out his challenge to Israel. David's heart was immediately stirred, not only because of his national pride but because the name of God was being put to open shame (see 17:26). Without fear, and to the surprise and chagrin of his fellow Israelites, David volunteered to accept the giant's challenge.

Saul tried to convince David he would not have a chance against Goliath. "You are not able to go against this Philistine to fight with him; for you are but a *youth* while he has been a warrior *from* his youth" (17:33). In other words, Saul believed David would virtually be committing suicide.

But Saul did not understand David. He did not know of his special skills in warfare or of his faith and trust in God. Neither did he comprehend God's special blessing upon this young man. When he saw that David was determined, he at first loaded him down with his own armor. But the young shepherd knew he couldn't function properly with the extra weight. Furthermore, he was unaccustomed to fighting under those conditions and he knew he couldn't possibly use his own weapon. He needed freedom of movement. He stripped off the armor and descended into the valley to face the giant in his simple shepherd garb, with nothing in his hands but a shepherd's staff, a sling and five smooth stones in a shepherd bag.

David Meets Goliath

Goliath must have been dumbfounded and mortified. Coming out to meet him with no protection—not even a shield bearer—was David. With no armor or helmet to cover his youthful appearance and his flowing red hair, Goliath recognized immediately he was facing an inexperienced youth. His anger reached a fever pitch and in his humiliation he cursed David. At this moment he may have thrown his helmet to the ground to face David with an unprotected head. Whatever transpired, his guard was down, and quick as a flash, before the Philistine knew what happened, the stone from David's sling pierced his forehead and the giant crashed to the ground, dead!

The Philistine army watched in horror as David severed Goliath's head from his body with the great warrior's own sword. Then the enemy fled, with the army of Israel in hot pursuit.

With this victory David entered a new era of his life, particularly in his relationship to the people of Israel. Unknown to him, however, he would have to travel a very difficult road before he finally became the recognized king of Israel.

GOLIATH'S PERSPECTIVE

This mighty Philistine warrior had a viewpoint of

himself and of life in general that stands out in bold relief in this fascinating story.

Goliath Placed Confidence in Himself and His Weapons

The Bible records it well: "He had a bronze helmet on his head, and he was clothed with scale armor which weighed five thousand shekels of bronze. He also had bronze greaves on his legs and a bronze javelin slung between his shoulders. And the shaft of his spear was like a weaver's beam, and the head of his spear weighed six hundred shekels of iron; his shield-carrier also walked before him" (17:5-7).

Goliath Was Proud and Arrogant

Goliath appeared before Israel with total self-confidence in his ability to defeat and kill any man who dared to face him on the battlefield. "I *defy* the ranks of Israel," he shouted (17:10).

Goliath Worshiped False Gods

When David approached him, Goliath cried out in anger: " 'Am I a dog, that you come to me with sticks?' And the Philistine cursed David *by his gods*" (17:43). Goliath, like all of his compatriots, did not worship the one, true God. The Philistines were deeply immeshed in the Canaanites' religious culture and worshiped false gods such as Dagon and Baalzebub (see Judg. 16:23,24; 1 Sam. 5:1-5; 2 Kings 1:2-6).

Because of Goliath's philosophy of life, he was easily deceived. When David approached Goliath with his shepherd garb, his staff and a sling in his hand, he threw Goliath off guard. The Philistine evidently only knew warfare of a certain kind. He was not prepared to face such a simple instrument as a slingshot. He only understood brute strength and how to use "a sword, a spear and a javelin" (1 Sam. 17:45). He could not imagine a sling being a deadly weapon.

In summary, Goliath's perspective represents a man of this world. He knew nothing of trusting God and honoring Him with his life. His confidence was purely in himself, in his military skills and in his protective armor. He did not comprehend, or at least refused to acknowledge, the one true God. And all of this, of course, made him extremely vulnerable to a man who did have skill, but who also had a dynamic relationship with the living God.

DAVID'S PERSPECTIVE

David's perspective on life in many respects was diametrically opposed to Goliath.

David Was Concerned About God's Reputation

The fact that Goliath was taunting Israel bothered David tremendously, not so much because of his national pride but because Israel represented God's chosen people. To attack Israel was to attack the *God* of Israel.

Furthermore, David wanted all people to know that it was God who helped Israel to win battles. He was concerned that neither he nor anyone in Israel ever take glory that belonged to the Lord. Thus he said, "This day the Lord will deliver you up into my hands ... *that all the earth may know* that there is a God in Israel, and *that all this assembly may know* that the Lord does not deliver by sword or by spear; *for the battle is the Lord's* and He will give you into our hands" (17:46,47).

David Had Confidence and Faith in God

When Saul tried to convince him he could never defeat Goliath, David's response was very revealing: "The Lord who delivered me from the paw of the lion and from the paw of the bear, He will deliver me from the hand of this Philistine" (17:37). And as he approached Goliath, he called out, "You come to me with a sword, a spear, and a javelin, but I come to you in *the name of the Lord of hosts*, the God of the armies of Israel, whom you have taunted" (17:45).

David Had Faith in Himself

David knew his own abilities and skills. When clothed in Saul's armor, he knew he could not function properly. He had great confidence in his ability to throw a stone with accuracy. But just in case he missed the first time, he had four more stones as back-up ammunition. In other words, David displayed a balance between his faith in God and in his own skills and abilities. Though he knew he was accurate, he did not want to take his accuracy for granted.

David Was Prepared for This Moment

David's skill with a sling was not an inherited ability. He no doubt spent many hours practicing out on the hillside while he was watching his father's sheep. And in Israel, a sling was really a secret weapon; many learned to use it with accuracy. In the book of Judges we read of 700 choice men who were left-handed and "each one could sling a stone at a hair and not miss" (Judg. 20:16).

TWENTIETH-CENTURY LESSONS

Though circumstances for people living today are much different than in Old Testament days, the two perspectives in this passage represent two classes of people at any given moment in history—believers and unbelievers; Christians and non-Christians; those who have put their trust in Jesus Christ for salvation, and those who have put their trust in themselves. Let's look more specifically at several direct applications.

How does this lesson apply to those who follow the way of Goliath? If Saul represents a carnal Christian who is in open rebellion against God, Goliath clearly represents the unbeliever who doesn't know God at all. Though this Philistine warrior certainly reflects this truth in the extreme, everything he did applies to the person who has not put his faith in Christ for salvation.

This was certainly true in my own life as a non-Christian. My trust was in myself—my abilities, my own talents, my own capabilities. Furthermore, my security was in my own accomplishments and in those material things I could accumulate in this world. And this, of course, led to pride and arrogance that stood in the way of recognizing God for who He really is and what He wanted to do in my life.

True, I wasn't pagan in that I denied God or Christ, but my false "gods" were myself, my friends and material things. That's basically all I had to live for. Though I believed in God, I had never bowed before Him, acknowledged my need for a Saviour, and accepted His free gift of eternal life. Consequently I was vulnerable to all kinds of failure. Because I trusted in myself, I was easily deceived and often disappointed in those things in which I put my faith for security.

What about you? Do you know Christ personally? Are you trusting in yourself and what you can do? Or are you trusting in Jesus Christ to be your personal Saviour? If not, why not accept Jesus Christ today? The following prayer will assist you. Pray it with meaning, and I assure you Jesus Christ will become your Saviour and your life will begin to change.

Father, like Goliath of old, I, _____ (your name), confess I have been trusting in myself to win the battles of life. I now humbly bow before you, acknowledge my sin of pride and self-righteousness and

I now put my faith in you to be my Saviour from sin. Come into my life and help me to change the direction of my life.

Signed _____

Date _____

How does this lesson apply to those who follow the way of David? David, of course, at this time in his life represents the Christian who is spiritual—the one who is following God with his whole heart and obeying His Word. How do you measure up? The following questions will help you:

1. How concerned am I about God's reputation? Many of us call ourselves "Christians," which means we claim to be followers of Jesus Christ. We have taken on His name. But how concerned are we that as His representatives we constantly and consistently bring honor to His name?

Note Paul's exhortation to the Corinthians: "So whether you eat or drink or whatever you do, do it all for the glory of God. Do not cause anyone to stumble, whether Jews, Greeks or the church of God—even as I try to please everybody in every way. For I am not seeking my own good but the good of many, so that they may be saved. Follow my example, as I follow the example of Christ" (1 Cor. 10:31—11:1).

2. How much do I trust God to help me achieve my goals? In our achievement-oriented culture it is very easy to go at our tasks totally in our own strength, not realizing how important it is to trust God in all things. I find myself bypassing God in the areas where I feel I can do things myself, and calling upon Him only when I'm in over my head and can't possibly make it on my own. God's desire is that we trust Him at all times. Note

God's will in this matter as it is spelled out in the book of Proverbs: "Trust in the Lord with all your heart, and do not lean on your own understanding. In all your ways acknowledge Him, and He will make your paths straight" (Prov. 3:5,6).

3. Do I balance faith in God with confidence in myself? The story of David facing Goliath beautifully balances this truth. On the one hand he knew the battle was the Lord's. On the other hand, he had confidence he could defeat Goliath with his unique skill with a slingshot.

Some Christians go to two extremes. Either they sit around and wait for God to fight their battles. Or they are out trying to win all by themselves. God wants us to balance this truth in our lives.

4. How prepared am I to do what God wants to achieve through me at any given moment? I'm convinced that God bypasses some Christians because they fail to become prepared for the situations where God wants to use them in special ways. David illustrates preparedness. He developed skill. And when he had an opportunity, God used that skill. How prepared are you for the time when God will want to do special things through your life?

5

DAVID FACES ANOTHER "GIANT"

1 Samuel 17:57,58; 18:5-18

When David slew Goliath, little did he realize that his heroic act would create a second "giant" far more fore-boding and difficult to confront and handle. The second "giant" was King Saul himself and the problem was jealousy. Goliath was clearly *an enemy*; Saul was supposedly *a friend*. And this made the problem particularly difficult for David. It was never completely solved until Saul died. But this is getting ahead of the story. What precipitated the problem? And what made it get worse?

DAVID'S POPULARITY (1 Sam. 18:1-5)

David's victory over Goliath created instant popularity for him. Everyone in Israel admired his great faith, courage and skill. People everywhere were immediately attracted to this young shepherd who dared to face the giant from Gath.

David and Jonathan

Among those most impressed by David was Jonathan, Saul's own son. In fact, a friendship developed between these two young men that is unequalled in biblical history. Respect and rapport quickly developed. As Jonathan listened in on the conversation between his father and David following the victory over Goliath (see 17:57,58), he recognized in this young man qualities of character he greatly admired. Jonathan's soul "was knit to the soul of David, and Jonathan loved him as himself" (18:1).

Because of his admiration for David, Jonathan "made a covenant" with his newfound friend. The covenant was reciprocal and mutual, for both Jonathan and David vowed to each other to be true and loyal friends the rest of their lives.

Jonathan sealed this contract with an act of kindness that is still considered in some parts of the world as the most significant honor one human being can bestow on another. When a prince clothes a subject with his own garments, there is no higher honor. And this Jonathan did for David. He "stripped himself of the robe that was on him and gave it to David, with his armor, including his sword and his bow and his belt" (18:4).

Saul Honors David

Following his victory over Goliath, Saul too viewed David in a different light. Though his actions may have been prompted more out of love for Jonathan than love for David, Saul also honored him. No longer was David merely his court musician and one of his armor-bearers, but he "set him over the men of war" (18:5). And even Saul's servants—a true test of popularity—admired David. Of all people, they could have become jealous, for David had been one of them. But they didn't and this is a reflection of how maturely David must have handled this situation.

But all was not well, especially within the heart of Saul. Though he had honored David outwardly, inwardly a struggle was developing that was soon to erupt and manifest itself with unbelievable ugliness.

SAUL'S JEALOUSY (1 Sam. 18:6-13)

For a time David held a record few men experience. On the surface at least, it appears that he had no enemies in Israel. But then it happened! Jealousy that had no doubt been brewing in the heart of Saul all along reared its ugly head. From the beginning David's popularity had threatened Saul.

David Is Praised

On the very day when the army returned from battle, large numbers of women "came out of all the cities of Israel, singing and dancing, to meet King Saul, with tambourines, with joy and with musical instruments" (18:6). And the words of their song triggered memories in Saul he wished he could forget: "Saul has slain his *thousands*, and David his *ten thousands*" (18:7).

Immediately Saul was enraged and suspicious. And the question he raised within himself clearly reveals why: "Now what more can he have but the kingdom?" (18:8). In other words, Saul saw prophetic fulfillment in David's popularity. Had not Samuel explicitly told Saul that the Lord had "sought out for Himself a man after His own heart" to replace him as king? (13:14). How could he forget? Even if he tried, the events that were unfolding before his eyes would not let him. And Saul once again took matters into his own hands and deliberately set out to thwart the will of God.

The severest form of jealousy usually involves two-dimensional popularity: the *popularity* of one person is superseded by *popularity* of another. And that is exactly what happened in Saul's case. In 1 Samuel 18, only David's popularity is described. But remember, to this point Saul had been Israel's national hero. When he was anointed king, everyone shouted, "Long live the king!" (10:24). And he too was a great warrior: "Now when Saul had taken the kingdom over Israel, he fought against all of his enemies on every side, against Moab, the sons of Ammon, Edom, the kings of Zobah, and the Philistines; and wherever he turned, he inflicted punishment. And he acted valiantly and defeated the Amalekites, and delivered Israel from the hands of those who plundered them" (14:47,48).

What happened when David became well-known in Israel, when he was lauded for his great exploits in battle? Succinctly stated, Saul's popularity was replaced by David's. And under most circumstances, unless the person being replaced is characterized by unusual maturity, being supplanted can lead to the worst kind of jealousy. And this is what happened to Saul.

There are at least three common emotions associated with jealousy and Saul experienced them all. First, he was *angry* (v. 8), then *suspicious* (v. 9), and finally, *fearful* (v. 12). As we've seen, Saul's anger surfaced when David was given more prominence in the hearts of the people than he himself. And this led to "suspicion" (v. 9). Saul kept a jealous eye on David and watched his every move.

Saul Threatens David

Unfortunately, Saul's jealousy led him to engage in irrational behavior. In uncontrollable rage, he looked for an opportunity to kill David, to eliminate the very object that was threatening his position. Twice Saul lifted his spear to hurl it at David while he was playing his harp, but on both occasions David managed to slip away.

In the midst of this irrational behavior, however, it seems Saul recognized that David was being guided by a power greater than his own. And he knew the source of that power, for he had at one time experienced it himself. Consequently his anger turned to fear. Thus we read that he was "*afraid* of David, for the Lord was with him but had departed from Saul" (18:12).

Saul's next action was to remove David from his presence. His motives for doing so are difficult to determine except from the larger context. In the immediate text we are simply told that "Saul removed him from his presence, and appointed him as his commander of a thousand; and he went out and came in before the people" (18:13). From this isolated statement we cannot determine if this was a promotion or a demotion. Personally, I think it was a promotion—but with an evil scheme. Saul, even in the midst of his emotional confusion, probably realized how horrible it would be in the eyes of all Israel should he personally kill David. He would destroy the object of his threat, but in doing so he would lose face with those he was trying to impress. In other words, he would destroy the popularity he was fighting to maintain and regain.

What were his alternatives? He could bow his heart before God, acknowledge that David was to be the successor and do what he could to prepare the way for the Lord's choice. Or he could continue to try to come up with a plan to eliminate David without destroying himself in the process. It's obvious he did not choose the first alternative. In what better way could he achieve his goal than to promote David, giving him more responsibility on the battlefield and making himself look good for doing so? Yet all the time Saul would be hoping that David would be killed by the Philistines.

This idea is supported by Saul's next action. He decided to give his older daughter to David to be his wife—*if* David would "be a *valiant* man . . . and fight the Lord's battles." This wording sounds noble and even spiritual, but beneath it was a diabolical scheme. Thus we read: "For Saul thought, 'My hand shall not be against him, but let the hand of the Philistine be against him' " (18:17). In other words, if the plan worked, Saul would gain recognition for promoting David and at the same time he would be eliminating David in an acceptable, legitimate way.

Obviously his plan backfired. God's blessing and protecting hand was continually upon David. He prospered "in all his ways for the Lord was with him." And "when Saul saw that he was prospering greatly, he dreaded him"—that is, he feared him even more. "But all Israel and Judah loved David, and he went out and came in before them" (18:14-16).

TWENTIETH-CENTURY LESSONS

Jealousy has always been a universal problem for all people. In fact it is an intricate part of our biological and psychological development. Jealousy first appears as a part of our emotional makeup between ages one and two and, ironically, the capacity to be jealous appears almost at the same time as the capacity to show affection toward other children. This, of course, is a very significant correlation. Saul's emotion of jealousy is also closely associated with other emotions he experienced —anger, suspicion and fear.

As a child grows and develops, God's plan is that he learn to understand his feelings and handle them constructively and maturely. Part of that plan involves Christian conversion and learning to experience God's power through His Word and His Holy Spirit.

But the fact is that most human beings are more *out*

of harmony with God's plan than *in* harmony. Even as Christians we battle the old nature that attempts to dominate us and cause us to sin. And giving way to jealous behavior is a constant temptation.

At this point it's important to realize that feelings themselves are not necessarily sin. It's what we do with these feelings that create the problem. And if we allow these emotions to persist and dominate us, they'll soon result in sinful actions. This is what James had in mind when he wrote that "each one is tempted when, by his own evil desire, he is dragged away and enticed. Then, after desire has conceived, it gives birth to sin" (Jas. 1:14,15).

What could Saul have done? In Saul's case, God certainly understood his feelings. Any man would have been threatened under the circumstances Saul faced. But God would also have helped Saul deal with his feelings, had he responded in the right way.

1. Saul could have dealt with his root problem. His main problem was pride and hardness of heart. He had never truly repented and shown remorse for his earlier disobedience. Here Saul was given another opportunity but he only hardened his heart more.

2. Saul could have turned to God for help. Of course, he didn't. As far as we know he didn't even ask God to change his heart attitude. Rather he took matters into his own hands. In fact, he actively fought against God's will.·

3. Saul could have sought help from others. His own son, Jonathan, could no doubt have helped him. But there, too, pride kept him from doing what was right.

4. Saul could have told David how he felt and sought his personal help. After all, if David could slay Goliath with God's help, maybe he could have helped Saul. But again, Saul made no effort to be honest with David.

Saul bypassed *all* the steps that are necessary when dealing with jealousy, or, for that matter, any negative emotion. He simply refused to face his problem. Consequently things went from bad to worse. And in cases like this, they always do.

What could David have done to help Saul? The more basic question is: What *did* David do? And the answer is, not much more than most people do today when facing a similar problem. With all due respect to David, who was indeed a man after God's heart facing a very difficult situation, there is one thing he could have done that he seemingly did not do. He could have approached this "giant" with the same faith and confidence he faced Goliath.

It doesn't appear that David even asked God for wisdom. Somehow this kind of problem is more difficult to turn over to the Lord. To cry out that "the battle is the Lord's" when facing a literal Goliath is one thing; to make the same statement when facing a person with an emotional problem is yet another. Especially when that emotional problem in some respects is working for us rather than against us, as it was in David's situation. Saul's immature behavior only enhanced David's behavior. Saul made David look "good."

I can think of times in my own life when I have fallen into this trap. When we threaten someone with our own skills and abilities, there is always a certain degree of emotional satisfaction. And if we are not extremely careful, we will use that situation for our own advantage. Unfortunately, David probably fell into this trap. The fact that he was "a man after God's own heart" did not exempt him from yielding to this kind of temptation.

A PERSONAL PROJECT
The following questions and guidelines are designed

to help you apply the lessons we can learn from this study.

Handling Personal Jealousy

1. Am I dealing with the root problem? (Do I really want to solve the problem?)

2. Have I sincerely turned to God for help?

3. Have I sought help from other mature Christians?

4. Have I shared my feelings with the other person involved, confessing my sin and asking for his forgiveness and prayers?

Handling Jealousy in Others

1. What are my motives? Am I using this person's weakness to enhance my own image?

2. What can I do to minimize this person's problems?

3. Do I pray for this person regularly?

4. If the person is a Christian, have I faced the problem on the basis of Matthew 7:3-5; Matthew 18:15-17; and Galatians 6:1,2?

6

DAVID'S "SOUL BROTHER"

1 Samuel 13:15-23; 14:1-23;
18:1-4 19:1-17; 20:1-42

What is true friendship? How is it generated? And how is it expressed? These questions, whether we verbalize them or not, are on the heart of every living human being. God created us to be social creatures and without friends our cup of life is only half full.

WHAT IS TRUE FRIENDSHIP? (1 Sam. 18:1)

The events in the life of David and Jonathan answer these questions better than any source I know of. In fact, the best definition of true friendship is found at the very beginning of their relationship when we read "that the *soul* of Jonathan *was knit* to the *soul* of David, and Jonathan *loved him as himself*" (18:1).

The word knit literally means "chained"; that is, the soul of Jonathan was chained to the soul of David. They were bound to each other in an inseparable relationship and union. In their minds and hearts they became one soul. They were in a true sense "soul brothers." Though the friendship was definitely initiated by Jonathan, it quickly became a reciprocal relationship. A friendship that is only one way is really no friendship at all.

WHAT PRECIPITATED THIS FRIENDSHIP?
(1 Sam. 13:15—14:23)

What brought this dynamic relationship between the son of Saul and the son of Jesse into being? Though a great social chasm originally existed between these two young men (David was just a shepherd boy and Jonathan a prince), they discovered in each other a common factor that made their friendship unique. They both were men after God's heart. They both had a dynamic relationship with their Lord. And when their souls were knit together as one it was not merely another human relationship. Rather it was a friendship that was also centered in God.

It seems that Jonathan was greatly impressed with David from the very moment the shepherd boy accepted the challenge to fight Goliath. Perhaps he had considered accepting this challenge himself, and on the same basis as David—that is, that the battle would have to be the Lord's. It may be that David simply beat him to it. You see, Jonathan's view of God's power was the same as David's. He had experienced it himself in a previous battle with the Philistines. And the parallels between Jonathan's experience and David's are quite obvious.

As pointed out in a previous chapter, the Philistines were uniquely equipped with shields, cloaks of armor, spears and javelins. Their economic specialization was iron and other metals. Furthermore, they had previously captured out of Israel every blacksmith they could find

so that the Israelites could not possibly equip themselves for battle (see 13:19). In fact, the problem was so
acute that every man in Israel had to rely on the Philistines to "sharpen his plowshare, his mattock, his axe,
and his goad" (13:20). In other words, Israel at this time
was economically dependent on the Philistines. They
couldn't even plow their fields and harvest their crops
without assistance from their enemies.

In the midst of this economic crisis and with Israel's
army unarmed, the Philistines decided to attack and to
finish the job once and for all. From a human perspective the children of Israel were doomed to disaster.
Three companies of Philistines approached from three
directions (see 13:17,18).

But there was in Israel a young man by the name of
Jonathan—Saul's son—who also believed that the battle
is the Lord's. He was among those few who had any
armor and weapons of warfare whatsoever. And without
consulting anyone, not even his father, he decided to
take on the whole Philistine army single-handedly (see
14:1). His only human assistant was his armor-bearer. In
many respects this was a greater challenge than taking
on Goliath.

But Jonathan, like David when he later went out to
meet Goliath, believed that God could win the battle for
him. This is why he said to the young man carrying his
armor, "Come and let us cross over to the garrison of
these uncircumcised; perhaps the Lord will work for us,
for the Lord is not restrained to save by many or by few"
(14:6). In other words, Jonathan believed in his heart
that if God so desired, he could deliver the whole Philistine army into his hands.

And the Lord did. After seeking God's will and getting a clear signal that the Lord would win this battle for
him (see 1 Sam. 14:8-11), he proceeded with great confidence, faith *and* humility. "Come up after me," he

called to his armor-bearer, "*for the Lord* has given them into the *hands of Israel*" (14:12).

God gave Jonathan unusual skill and ability as he approached the Philistines. Furthermore, He caused a gigantic "trembling in the camp, in the field, and among all the people. Even the garrison and the raiders trembled, and the earth quaked so that it became a great trembling" (14:15).

The Philistines were so shook up—literally and emotionally—that they fled with the Israelites in hot pursuit. That day the "Lord delivered Israel" (14:23). It was a miraculous victory. God honored Jonathan's faith. In his heart, Jonathan knew the battle had been the Lord's.

And that day as Jonathan stood in the wings watching David accept Goliath's challenge and, single-handedly, without Saul's armor, slay the giant, memories of his own experiences must have flooded his mind and heart. There was immediate identification with David's experience and Jonathan felt his soul strangely drawn to this new and God-honoring Hebrew brother. They had something in common, something very important. They both were men whose hearts were in tune with God. They knew God personally and understood His greatness. And perhaps more important than anything, they had a clear understanding of God's love and commitment to Israel. Both of them knew without a shadow of doubt that they were fighting the Lord's battle, not their own. There was no way they could have succeeded in their own strength.

It's important then to realize that this friendship was no ordinary friendship. True, all the human elements were there—emotion, respect and commitment—but interweaving all of these human factors was a divine dimension that made this Old Testament friendship one of the most significant relationships ever recorded in human history.

HOW WAS THIS FRIENDSHIP EXPRESSED?
(1 Sam. 18:1-4; 19:1—20:42)

It's one thing to talk about "friendship"; it's another to demonstrate it. And Jonathan, particularly, exemplifies the hallmarks of genuine friendship in his relationship with David.

Jonathan Honored David Above Himself

Jonathan, since he initiated this friendship, also took the lead in establishing this friendship on a solid foundation. In fact, since he was a prince and David a subject, there was no other alternative but to take the first step. He "stripped himself of the robe that was on him [his royal robe] and gave it to David, with his armor, including his sword and his bow and his belt" (18:4).

To honor another person above yourself when you are social equals is one thing; to do so in Jonathan's situation is yet another. Here was a son of a king honoring the son of a shepherd—above himself. Jonathan apparently recognized in David a man who had even greater personal courage and confidence in God than he himself. He had done what Jonathan had hesitated to do— and without armor, shield or sword.

At this moment Jonathan knew full well the implications of what he was doing. Was he not heir to the throne of Israel? By all human conditions, he was. But he was willing to step aside to make way for his *friend*, for he truly believed that David could do the job better than he could. And this attitude in Jonathan is verified later when he said to David: "You will be king over Israel and I will be next to you" (23:17).

Jonathan Served as a Faithful Intercessor

Saul's jealousy of David continued to flare. Subtly he tried various ways to kill him, but each time he failed. Finally he made it an open issue. He told Jonathan and all his servants about his evil desire (see 19:1).

Jonathan immediately went to work to thwart his father's plan. First, he warned David (see 19:2). Then he went directly to his father and began to intercede for his beloved friend. "Do not let the king sin against his servant David," he pleaded. "He has not sinned against you." In fact, Jonathan continued, "his deeds have been very beneficial to you. For he took his life in his hand and struck the Philistine, and the Lord brought about a great deliverance for all Israel; you saw it and rejoiced. Why then will you sin against innocent blood, by putting David to death without a cause?" (19:4-6).

Jonathan's act of love paid off, at least temporarily. Saul changed his mind and promised Jonathan he would not kill David. And Jonathan, true friend that he was, personally escorted David back into Saul's presence once again to serve the king both as his private musician and as an army officer (see 19:7).

Jonathan Continued to Be Faithful to David

Jonathan's success in building a bridge between his father and David was only temporary. In a fit of rage, while David was playing his harp, Saul once again tried to pin David to the wall. Fortunately he missed and David "slipped away out of Saul's presence" (19:10).

Saul's next move was to send a delegation to David's house to kill him. But David, with the help of his wife Michal, again escaped (see 19:11-17).

After visiting Samuel in Ramah, David returned to consult with Jonathan. At this point in David's life we see a very emotionally disturbed and threatened man. He feared for his life. Based on previous experience, David felt he could no longer trust Jonathan's interpretation of Saul's motives. Not that he didn't trust the integrity of his friend, but he believed Saul was no longer telling Jonathan the truth (see 20:3).

But Jonathan proved faithful again. He was willing to do *anything* David asked (see 20:4). And to test Saul's motives, they agreed that David would be absent from his regularly scheduled meal with Saul. If the king reacted with anger, they would know Saul had not changed.

The results were as David had predicted. In fact Saul was so angry he tried to kill his own son Jonathan, accusing him of protecting David. His words were cruel and harsh: "You son of a perverse, rebellious woman!" he screamed at Jonathan. "Do I not know that you are choosing the son of Jesse to your own shame and to the shame of your mother's nakedness? For as long as the son of Jesse lives on the earth, neither you nor your kingdom will be established. Therefore now, send and bring him to me, for he must surely die" (20:30,31).

Once again Jonathan interceded for David, but to no avail. The king "hurled his spear at him to strike him down." And at that moment Jonathan knew for sure "that his father had decided to put David to death" (20:33). What had been periodic outbursts of anger had turned into a determined plot. David would no longer be able to trust Saul. From this point forward he would be a fugitive.

David's heart was broken when Jonathan told him what had happened. They both knew it meant separation. Jonathan had no choice but to be loyal to his father, and David would certainly have had it no other way. But the decision was a difficult one for both of them. They wept and kissed each other as they parted, and though they would see very little of each other from that moment onward, they were never separated in their hearts. They were true friends, and *true* friends can never be separated.

A NEW TESTAMENT PARALLEL
In many respects the relationship between David and

Jonathan constitutes an Old Testament picture of a New Testament reality—the relationships in the Body of Christ. What characterized this *unique* friendship in Israel was to be a *norm* in the church.

Note first the essence of this relationship. David and Jonathan were of "one soul." Compare this reality with the following New Testament references to relationships that should exist in the Body of Christ:

"All the believers [in Jerusalem] were *one* in heart and mind" (Acts 4:32).

"May the God who gives endurance and encouragement give you a spirit of unity among yourselves as you follow Christ Jesus, so that with *one heart and mouth* you may glorify the God and Father of our Lord Jesus Christ" (Rom. 15:5).

"Be of one mind" (2 Cor. 13:11).

"Stand firm in *one spirit*, contending as *one man*" (Phil. 1:27).

"Make my joy complete by being *like-minded*, having the same love, being *one* in spirit and purpose" (Phil. 2:2).

Note second that David and Jonathan loved each other as they loved themselves. Compare this reality to the following New Testament injunctions:

"Be devoted to one another in brotherly love" (Rom. 12:10).

"Love your neighbor as yourself" (Rom. 13:9).

"Follow the way of love" (1 Cor. 14:1).

"Love your neighbor as yourself" (Gal. 5:14).

"Keep on loving each other as brothers" (Heb. 13:1).

"Love one another deeply, with all your hearts" (1 Pet. 1:22).

It is very clear from these selected Scriptures, and many more, that the relationship between David and Jonathan was prophetic. In Jesus Christ, Christian brothers and sisters have the potential for true and enduring friendships that can never be equalled on this earth. True, all human beings can experience "friendship" because we are made in God's image. But only Christians have the potential for the quality of relationship that existed between David and Jonathan. The reason is that this relationship was focused both in God and man. And in Christ, we can experience the same depth of commitment to each other.

Note finally that the way in which their friendship was expressed parallels New Testament injunctions to members of Christ's body:

DAVID AND JONATHAN'S RELATIONSHIP	RELATIONSHIPS WITHIN CHRIST'S BODY
1. Jonathan honored David above himself.	1. Paul wrote to the Romans: "Honor one another above yourselves" (Rom. 12:10).
2. Jonathan served as a faithful intercessor. He was devoted to David, served him and did everything he could to help David build a relationship with his father.	2. Paul wrote: "Be devoted to one another" (Rom. 12:10). "Serve one another in love" (Gal. 5:13). "If one part suffers, every part suffers with it" (1 Cor. 12:26).
3. Jonathan continued to be faithful to David no matter what the circumstances cost him personally. His life was in jeopardy when he tried to defend David's absence.	3. John wrote in his First Epistle: "This is how we know what love is: Jesus Christ laid down his life for us. And we ought to lay down our lives for our brothers" (1 John 3:16).

A PERSONAL PROJECT

1. What kind of friend am I to other Christians generally?

☐ Do I do all I can to be one with other believers?

☐ Do I honor others above myself?

☐ Am I loyal to my friends no matter what the cost to me personally?

☐ How willing would I be to lay my own life on the line for a Christian brother or sister?

2. What kind of friend am I to those closest to me: my parents, my wife, my husband, my children, my brothers and sisters?

NOTE: Sometimes the most difficult place to be a *true friend* is in our own homes.

3. Select one area in your life where you feel you need to improve your friendship with another Christian. Then ask God to help you carry out your goal.

7

FROM
FAITH
TO
FEAR

1 Samuel 19:18-24; 20:1-42; 21;1-15;
Psalm 34

"I find it tremendously comforting," writes Dr. Alan Redpath, "that the Bible never flatters its heroes. It tells the truth about them no matter how unpleasant it may be, so that in considering what is taking place in the shaping of their character we have available all the facts clearly that we may study them."[1] This is particularly obvious in a study of David's life. Though he was called a "man after God's own heart," yet he had serious character weaknesses that are clearly described in the Word of God.

Thus far in our survey of David's life we have noticed his strengths. He *was* a man after God's heart. The Spirit of the Lord was upon him mightily. Against impossible

73

odds, he faced Goliath and slew him, which was only the beginning of his great exploits in battle against the Philistines. He became known in Israel as a man of unusual courage and great faith in God.

But all was not well in David's heart and life. A change was gradually taking place. Little by little his faith in God's protection was being replaced by fear of what man could do to him. And that man, of course, was King Saul.

From a human perspective, David's fear is understandable, even predictable. He had served Saul as one of his armor-bearers and as his personal musician. At one time the king had demonstrated great love toward him (see 16:21). But when David was honored by the people of Israel for his great victory over Goliath, Saul's love turned to jealousy, anger and suspicion. He actually looked for an opportunity to kill David.

Foiled in his attempts, Saul planned David's death on the battlefield by giving him greater military responsibility, but to no avail. Repeatedly, he tried to "pin David to the wall" with his spear. But once again David escaped and took refuge in his home. But Saul's anger was now relentless. He sent his men to kill David. But David, with his wife's help, escaped through a window and fled.

Saul's attempts on David's life were becoming more frequent and intense. It was no longer a private scheme but a public strategy. And no one, including God Himself, would blame David for fleeing from Saul's presence. It was the only sensible thing to do.

But *how* David responded to these pressures and, more significant, how he responded to God's protection from Saul is yet another matter. Rather than trusting the Lord as he had done so frequently in difficult situations, he began to lose his spiritual and emotional bearings. As we'll see, David ignored God's protection and took matters into his own hands. And when he did, things went from bad to worse.

DAVID IGNORES GOD'S PROTECTION
(1 Sam. 19:18-24)

When David slipped out of his house through a window and escaped from Saul's men, he fled to Ramah (see 19:18). There he met and talked with the prophet Samuel. David no doubt poured out his fears and frustrations to this old man who had originally anointed him to be the second king of Israel. Unfortunately it doesn't appear that Samuel was much help. It may be that he was so filled with fear of Saul himself, that he was unable to encourage David or help restore his faith.[2]

Though it is not clear what transpired between David and Samuel, it is perfectly obvious from the text of Scripture that God was willing and able to protect David from Saul, just as he had delivered him from his enemies on many previous occasions. When Saul heard that David was at Ramah, immediately he sent his men to capture David. When they arrived, they saw Samuel and a company of prophets prophesying before God. And lo and behold, the Spirit of the Lord came upon Saul's men and they also began to prophesy. Though we cannot be sure of all the dynamics involved, evidently these men were supernaturally thwarted by God in carrying out Saul's orders (see 19:20).

When Saul heard what had happened, he sent more men. The same thing transpired. And in his unabated determination, he sent a third company of men, but only to hear that the Spirit of God came upon them as well and thwarted their efforts (see 19:21).

Saul's next move was to go to Ramah himself and capture David personally. But when he arrived, the Spirit of God came upon him also and so overpowered him that he lost complete control of his own will and prophesied along with the other prophets (see 19:23,24). In these events, God was communicating two very important messages.

God Was Still Reaching Out to Saul

When the Spirit of God came upon Saul and his men, the Lord was certainly reminding Saul of a very special event that had transpired earlier in his life. Soon after he was anointed king, "the Spirit of God came upon him mightily, so that he prophesied among" the prophets (10:6,9,10). In fact the question the people asked at that time was the same as the question they asked again: "Is Saul also among the prophets?" (10:11; 19:24).

There was no way for Saul to miss the divine message: he was not just fighting David; he was fighting God. And furthermore God was still able to change Saul's heart and life permanently, should he let Him.

God Would Deliver David

The second message, perhaps the most significant in this passage, was for David. God could and would protect and deliver David from Saul. And before David's eyes, the Lord visually and dramatically demonstrated this fact. Without God's permission, Saul and his men could not touch David. In these events, God was showing David that He would protect him just as He had when David confronted Goliath.

DAVID TAKES MATTERS INTO HIS OWN HANDS (1 Sam. 20:1-42; 21:1-15)

It's quite clear from Scripture that David's response to God's intervention on his behalf was anything but positive. As we noted in our previous lesson, when David returned to talk to his friend Jonathan, he was a very emotionally and spiritually disturbed young man. His questions—"What have I done? What is my iniquity?

And what is my sin before your father, that he is seeking my life?" (20:1)—reflect confusion, doubt, and tremendous anxiety. And when Jonathan tried to reassure him, his response was skeptical and nervous.

In all fairness to David, it must be noted that he was right about Saul. Jonathan *was* deceived. David may have been frightened and anxious but he had an accurate picture of his relationship with the king of Israel. David was desperately hated and Saul was determined to kill him.

David's problem, however, focused on the fact that he was not trusting God to protect and deliver him. He had lost perspective on the past. What about "the lion," "the bear" and "the giant Goliath"? Seemingly, he even ignored totally what had just transpired in Ramah. Lost in a maze of his present circumstances, he proceeded to take matters into his own hands. The results were tragic!

David's First Scheme

The essence of David's plan is recorded in chapter 20, verses 5-7: "Behold, tomorrow is the new moon, and I ought to sit down to eat with the king. But let me go, that I may hide myself in the field until the third evening. If your father misses me at all, then say, 'David earnestly asked leave of me to run to Bethlehem his city, because it is the yearly sacrifice there for the whole family.' If he says, 'It is good,' your servant shall be safe; but if he is very angry, know that he has decided on evil."

David didn't consult the Lord at all. In fact, the Lord's name is not even mentioned in the plan.

How opposite from David's attitude and actions when he faced Goliath! At that time he said to Saul with great confidence, "*The Lord* who delivered me from the paw of the lion and from the paw of the bear, He will deliver me from the hand of this Philistine" (1 Sam. 17:37). And when he actually encountered the giant face to face

David shouted, "I come to you *in the name of the Lord of hosts*, the *God* of the armies of Israel .... This day the *Lord* will deliver you up into my hands, ... that all the earth may know that there is a *God* in Israel, and that all the assembly may know that the *Lord* does not deliver by sword or by spear; for the *battle is the Lord's* and *He* will give you into our hands" (17:45-47).

What happened to David's God-consciousness? Somehow, some way, he lost his spiritual perspective. Rather than saying to Jonathan that day, "This struggle between your father and me *is the Lord's. He* will deliver me just as He did in Ramah," he came up with his own scheme, leaving God out of the picture.

There was an element of dishonesty in David's strategy. True, he *may* have ultimately planned to go to Bethlehem to sacrifice with his family, but there's no evidence he ever did or that he really planned to go. Furthermore, he asked Jonathan to give the impression he had already gone to Bethlehem (see 20:27-29), when in reality he was waiting "in the field" for a report on Saul's behavior (20:24).

But this was just the beginning of David's falsification. One lie often leads to another, and this is exactly what happened to David.

David's Second Scheme

Though David's scheme was purely a human strategy, it achieved its purpose. Saul's anger was so uncontrolled when he discovered that David was not coming to his special luncheon that he attempted to kill Jonathan instead (see 20:33). But his son escaped and went out into the field to communicate the bad news to his beloved friend. In David's mind, he had no choice. Once again he fled, this time to Nob where the Tabernacle was.

The priest, Ahimelech, was surprised to see David, especially since he was alone (see 21:1). And David, again taking matters into his own hands, took advantage of Ahimelech's surprise and quickly fabricated another story. "The king has commissioned me with a matter, and has said to me, 'Let no one know anything about the matter on which I am sending you and with which I have commissioned you' " (21:2). In other words, "I'm alone because I'm on a secret mission for the king."

But this time things didn't work out as nicely as David had planned. Though he fooled Ahimelech, it just so happened that one of Saul's chief shepherds, Doeg the Edomite, was also in Nob that same day and saw David. Later he reported what he had seen and the word got back to Saul.

The results of David's sin in this case were tragic. Saul immediately called for Ahimelech and his whole family of priests. The king was irate and irrational. In his paranoid condition he accused Ahimelech of protecting David and helping him to escape. No explanation would suffice. Ahimelech's innocence was totally ignored and Saul ordered Ahimelech's death as well as the death of all the priests who were present that day—a total of 85 men (see 22:18). Also, he ordered an attack on the city of Nob and struck "both men and women, children and infants; also oxen, donkeys, and sheep" (22:19).

All of this happened because David took matters into his own hands and lied. Later he acknowledged to a lone survivor, Abiathar, that he, personally, had "brought about the death of every person" in Nob (22:22,23). One sin led to another and seriously affected many others. David escaped with his scheme but in the process he caused the death of hundreds of innocent people. What a price to have to pay for his disobedience and lack of trust in God!

David's Third Scheme
Before David learned from his mistakes, in fact before

he even learned about the death of the people in Nob, he engaged in still another scheme. This time, his behavior was even more bizarre and pathetic.

David left Nob and headed into enemy territory, hoping he no longer would be recognized as a warrior in Israel. But he was wrong. He was immediately identified by the servants of Achish, king of Gath (see 21:10,11).

David's anxiety now reached almost unbearable proportions. We're told he "greatly feared Achish" (21:12). And what we see next as a result of this fear is a person who is hardly recognizable when compared with the man of God we've studied about in previous lessons. David panicked and feigned madness. In a pathetic demonstration of insanity he "scribbled on the doors of the gate, and let saliva run down into his beard" (21:13).

Again, David's scheme worked. He escaped injury. But finding himself in a lonely cave, he no doubt began to reflect on his bizarre and sinful behavior. Once again he began to focus his heart and mind on the Lord. He had learned a very hard lesson.

DAVID LEARNS A DIFFICULT BUT DYNAMIC LESSON (Ps. 34)

Following his experience in enemy territory, David wrote a psalm, Psalm 34, that reflects a much different picture than what we've seen thus far. Once again we see a man after God's heart—a man who trusted in the Lord to provide for him and to deliver him from his enemies.

At this juncture the psalm is self-explanatory.

David's focus is back on God and His power, not on himself and his own ability. He had learned a very difficult but dynamic lesson and he wanted to warn others so they would not make the same mistake.

I will bless the **Lord** *at all times;*
His *praise shall continually be in my mouth.*
My soul shall make its boast **in the Lord;**

The humble shall hear it and rejoice.
O magnify the **Lord** *with me,*
And let us exalt **His name** *together.*

I sought the **Lord,** *and* **He** *answered me,*
And delivered me from all my **fears.**
They looked to **Him** *and were radiant,*
And their faces shall never be ashamed.
This poor man cried and the **Lord** *heard him;*
And saved him out of all his troubles.
The angel of the **Lord** *encamps around those who*
    fear **Him,**
And rescues them.

O taste and see that the **Lord** *is good;*
How blessed is the man who takes refuge in **Him!**
O fear the **Lord,** *you His saints;*
For to those who fear **Him,** *there is no want.*
The young lions do lack and suffer hunger;
But they who seek the **Lord** *shall not be in*
    want of any good thing.
Come, you children, listen to me;
I will teach you the fear of the Lord.
Who is the man who desires life,
And loves length of days that he may see good?
Keep your tongue from evil,
And your lips from speaking deceit.
Depart from evil, and do good;
Seek peace, and pursue it.

The **eyes of the Lord** *are toward the righteous,*
And His ears are open to their cry.
The **face of the Lord** *is against evildoers,*
To cut off the memory of them from the earth.
The righteous cry and the **Lord** *hears,*
And delivers them out of all their troubles.

The Lord is near to the brokenhearted,
And saves those who are crushed in spirit.

Many are the afflictions of the righteous;
But the Lord delivers him out of them all.
He keeps all his bones;
Not one of them is broken.
Evil shall slay the wicked;
And those who hate the righteous will
* be condemned.*
The Lord redeems the soul of His servants;
And none of those who take refuge in Him will
* be condemned.*
(Ps. 34:1-22)

A TWENTIETH-CENTURY LESSON

During this period in David's life he was spiritually and emotionally confused. His present circumstances and pressures became a maze of bewilderment. He couldn't "see the forest for the trees." Somehow he couldn't seem to remember either God's previous promises or provisions. And even God's immediate care and concern were blurred and out of focus. Rather than responding to God's supernatural help by trusting the Lord to always help him escape Saul's death traps, David took matters into his own hands. He schemed and connived.

But as usually happens in such cases, matters got worse. True, each time David's scheme helped him escape death. But the results were tragic. Because of his first scheme, David and his beloved friend Jonathan were separated, never to see each other again. His second scheme cost many innocent people their lives and brought guilt into his own life. And his third scheme stands out in bold relief as a miserable testimony before the pagan king of Gath and his people.

What about you? Have you ever lost perspective, unable to remember God's promises and provisions in your own life? Do even the Lord's daily miracles in your own life, such as health and strength, sometimes seem unrelated to the supernatural? Have you ever taken matters into your own hands and made a mess of things? It's at times like these that we too hurt those closest to us, cause innocent people to suffer and bring reproach on the name of Jesus Christ.

Note, too, that it's at times like these that we begin to allow dishonesty to creep into our lives. Our first scheme may include just a little white lie, but our next step leads to a boldfaced one. And finally, before we know it, we're in so deep we're feigning something we are not. We've moved from telling lies to living them.

But it's at this point we need to remember David's example. True, he blew it. He failed God miserably. But he turned from his sin and once again acknowledged the Lord. Maybe you too are a man, woman or a young person after God's heart. But you've blown it also. In a state of anxiety and fear you've taken matters into your own hands. In the process, you've been dishonest and matters have gone from bad to worse. You know you're living out of the will of God.

Remember David. In a lonely cave, he came to his senses. He refocused his life. He confessed his sin. And so can you—wherever you find yourself. You may not be in a lonely cave, but there's a strange aloneness in your heart because of your sin and guilt. Remember that there is forgiveness in Jesus Christ. The Saviour has already made atonement for your sins. Believe it, accept it and appropriate that forgiveness by acknowledging your sin and turning from it (see 1 John 1:9).

A FINAL WORD

Remember that trusting God does not mean we are

not responsible. When David took on the giant Goliath, he had a scheme, a plan. But that plan was made in prayer and undergirding faith. David knew he could do nothing without God's help. And furthermore, at that time David was straightforward and honest. He gave glory and honor to God.

The following New Testament verses present God's standard in our relationships with others. How does your life measure up? Underscore any area where you fall short. If you have failed God in some area of your life, acknowledge your sin, ask God's forgiveness and become a different person.

• "Therefore, each of you must put off falsehood and speak truthfully to his neighbor, for we are all members of one body" (Eph. 4:25).

• "Make it your ambition to lead a quiet life, to mind your own business and to work with your hands, just as we told you, so that your daily life may win the respect of outsiders and so that you will not be dependent upon anybody" (1 Thess. 4:11,12).

• "So whether you eat or drink or whatever you do, do it all for the glory of God. Do not cause anyone to stumble, whether Jews, Greeks or the Church of God" (1 Cor. 10:31,32).

• "Live such good lives among the pagans that, though they accuse you of doing wrong, they may see your good deeds and glorify God on the day he visits us" (1 Pet. 2:12).

• "Be wise in the way you act toward outsiders; make the most of every opportunity. Let your conversation be always full of grace, seasoned with salt, so that you may know how to answer everyone" (Col. 4:5,6).

A PERSONAL PROJECT
Since deciding to acknowledge your sin and live your life according to God's plan, you too may wish to write

a psalm reflecting the difference in your life, just as
David did.

Notes

1. Alan Redpath, *The Making of a Man of God* (Westwood, NJ: Fleming H. Revell, 1957), p. 67.
2. Note in 1 Samuel 15:35 that Samuel, following his message of judgment on Saul, "did not see Saul again until the day of his death." We're also told that "Samuel grieved over Saul." And later in 1 Samuel 16:2 we are told that Samuel was so fearful of Saul that he thought the king might kill him. Evidently, this was Samuel's feelings until the day he died. It stands to reason then that Samuel probably offered David very little encouragement and help.

8

FROM FEAR TO FAITH

*1 Samuel 23;
Psalms 27; 31*

Following David's period of deep distress and fear, which caused him to take matters into his own hands and woefully make a mess of things, he emerged from the cave of Adullam a different man. While hiding there from Saul, he had many quiet hours to think and reflect on his bizarre and deceitful behavior. It was there he no doubt had a unique encounter with his Lord.

DAVID'S DIVINE PERSPECTIVES (1 Sam. 23:1-14)

Though a much different environment from the hillsides of Judea where David cared for his father's sheep and communicated with his Maker, the dark cave of Adullam provided an aura in which to realize the "darkness" that had captured his own soul. Once again the true light of God's revelation brightened his outlook on life and brought him a sense of inner security. Once again David's mind and heart were focused on the Lord rather than on his own skills and abilities. And once again he faced the threat to the lives of the children of Israel and to his own life with a divine perspective. This is very clear in two incidents we have recorded for us in 1 Samuel 23.

Encounter with the Philistines

Sometime soon after David's renewed perspective, he received word that the Philistines had attacked Israel at Keilah (23:1). David's response to the situation reflects the man who had often on previous occasions amazed and thrilled the hearts of his people—the David who faced the lion and the bear with great confidence in God, the David who slew Goliath and won many victories over the Philistines. "*So David inquired of the Lord*, saying, 'Shall I go and attack these Philistines?' And the Lord said to David, 'Go and attack the Philistines, and deliver Keilah' " (23:2).

David's 400 men—a motley crew—responded to this challenge with tremendous hesitation and fear. "Behold," they said, "we are afraid here in Judah. How much more then if we go to Keilah against the ranks of the Philistines?" (23:3).

From a human perspective we can understand why these men were so fearful. First, they weren't first class soldiers. In fact, their classification was "3-D." Scripture records that "everyone who was in *distress*, and everyone who was in *debt*, and everyone who was *discontented*, gathered to" join David in the cave of Adullam (22:2).

What a nucleus for an army! They were already a fearful lot—outlaws, if you will, on the run because of their rebellion against Saul's government. They were men who were in debt and unable to pay their debtors, and men whose hearts were already embittered and angry because of what they felt were injustices in their society. Their anxiety and fear when David issued an order to attack the Philistine army in Keilah are understandable.

But secondly, they were few in number and ill equipped compared with their enemy. Humanly speaking they would be foolish to attack the well-armed and well-trained Philistines.

David's response to their reactions reflects how well he had learned his lesson. Fear begets fear, especially in a person who is anxious to begin with. Had David not regained his spiritual and emotional bearings he would have succumbed and regressed to his previous behavior. I'm sure David in his humanness flashed back to his earlier obsessions and fears. But rather than being *pulled down* by his men's pessimism, he *looked up* to the Lord, "Then David inquired of the Lord once more." And once again, "the Lord answered him and said, 'Arise, go down to Keilah, for I will give the Philistines into your hands' " (23:4).

David, reassured by God's promise, boldly led his men to Keilah and delivered his fellow Israelites from the Philistines. In his personal relationship with God, he had moved from fear to faith. The hand of God was upon David as before. Once again he was functioning with the divine perspective on how to solve life's problems.

Encounter with Saul

Saul's system of espionage was continually at work in tracking David. Word soon got back to the king that David was in Keilah. Immediately, he commissioned his soldiers "to go down to Keilah to besiege David and his men" (23:8).

But David's renewed faith was not only revealed in his dealings with the Philistines but also in his relationship with Saul. As soon as he heard of the king's plot, he once again consulted the Lord, asking some very specific questions: "O Lord God of Israel, Thy servant has heard for certain that Saul is seeking to come to Keilah to destroy the city on my account. Will the men of Keilah surrender me into his hand? Will Saul come down just as Thy servant has heard? O Lord God of Israel, I pray, tell Thy servant" (23:10-12).

Evidently David was not willing to act on man's word alone. The rumor may or may not have been true. Furthermore, some of Saul's previous attempts had been thwarted. David wanted to know for sure if he would indeed come to Keilah and what would happen.

God's answer to David's prayer was straightforward. David asked a specific question and he got a specific answer. "And the Lord said, 'He will come down'" (23:11).

God had answered his second question but not his first. So David asked the first one again. David wanted to know what would actually happen if he remained inside the walls of the city. Thus David restated his question: "Will the men of Keilah surrender me and my men into the hands of Saul?" Again the Lord's answer was specific: "They will surrender you" (23:12).

David and his men, now numbering about 600, fled Keilah. And when the king discovered that David had left the city he changed his mind and halted his attack.

But Saul would not give up. He was determined to take David's life. So he continued his search. But it was to no avail. As long as David trusted the Lord and sought His will and guidance, he continually escapd from Saul's death traps. Thus we read that Saul "sought him every day, but God did not deliver him into his hand" (23:14).

DAVID'S DIVINE PERSPECTIVE IN THE PSALMS
(Pss. 27;31)

During this renewal period of faith and confidence in God, David wrote several psalms reflecting his experience with the Lord.

Psalms 27 and 31 certainly speak of his new perspective and likely were among those penned during this period in David's life. Listen to the opening lines in each of these psalms and note how they reflect his confidence and faith in God:

> *The Lord is my light and my salvation;*
> *Whom shall I fear?*
> *The Lord is the defense of my life;*
> *Whom shall I dread?*
> *When evildoers came upon me to devour my flesh,*
> *My adversaries and my enemies, they stumbled*
> *   and fell.*
> *Though a host encamp against me,*
> *My heart will not fear;*
> *Though war arise against me,*
> *In spite of this I shall be confident.*
> (27:1-3)

> *In Thee, O Lord, I have taken refuge;*
> *Let me never be ashamed;*
> *In Thy righteousness deliver me.*
> *Incline Thine ear to me, rescue me quickly;*
> *Be Thou to me a rock of strength,*
> *A stronghold to save me.*
> *For Thou art my rock and my fortress;*
> *For Thy name's sake Thou wilt lead me*
> *   and guide me.*
> *Thou wilt pull me out of the net which they have*
> *   secretly laid for me;*
> *For Thou art my strength.*

Into Thy hand I commit my spirit;
Thou hast ransomed me, O Lord, God of truth.
(31:1-5)

TWENTIETH-CENTURY LESSONS

How can we as Christians facing twentieth-century problems learn to trust God? How can we develop a divine perspective on life?

We must learn from past mistakes. This was one of David's secrets. Rather than allowing his failures to hold him captive, he turned to God. Rather than wallowing in self-pity, he turned his eyes heavenward. Rather than continuing to repeat old patterns, he refocused his attitudes and behavior.

What about you? Are you learning from past mistakes or are you repeating them? Are you locked into the past or are you allowing God to break the shackles of failure that have bound you? Remember, the Lord wants to be your light and your salvation—just as He was David's. He will be the defense of your life. You need not fear. Trust Him! Step out in faith believing that He will be your source of strength no matter what the problem.

We must seek His will through His Word. One very significant lesson David learned was that he could not solve his problems by himself. He needed God's wisdom. And so do you.

In difficult days God often spoke directly to some of His key leaders. In fact David had direct access to God. He actually conversed with God as did Moses and Abraham.

Today God has spoken to us through the Bible. We have His Word. And in the Scriptures He reveals His will for all mankind. Furthermore, it is through His Word that we develop faith. Thus Paul wrote: "Faith

91

comes from hearing the message, and the message is heard through the word of Christ" (Rom. 10:17).

How consistent are you in learning more and more of His Word? As you do you will learn more and more of His will for your life. Are you studying it regularly, preferably daily? Do you consult the Scriptures when you face problems? When you are making important decisions? Remember the words of Joshua: "This book of the law shall not depart from your mouth, but you shall meditate on it day and night, so that you may be careful to do according to all that is written in it; for *then* you will make your way prosperous, and then you will have success" (Josh. 1:8).

We must seek His will through prayer. David did not hesitate to ask God specific questions. When he did, he got specific answers. Though normally God does not speak directly to His children as He did with certain select leaders of old, He does answer prayer. He speaks through His revealed Word. He speaks through circumstances. And He speaks through other members of the Body of Christ. Remember Paul's exhortation to the Philippians: "Do not be anxious about anything, but in everything, by prayer and petition, with thanksgiving, present your requests to God. And the peace of God, which transcends all understanding, will guard your hearts and your minds in Christ Jesus" (Phil. 4:6,7).

Remember too the words of James, which are perhaps even more relevant to David's situation and example: "Consider it pure joy, my brothers, whenever you face trials of many kinds, because you know that the testing of your faith develops perseverance. Perseverance must finish its work so that you may be mature and complete, not lacking anything. If any of you lacks wisdom, he should ask God, who gives generously to all without finding fault, and it will be given to him. But when he asks, he must believe and not doubt, because he who doubts is like a wave of the sea, blown and tossed by the wind. That man should not think he will receive anything from the Lord; he is a doubleminded man, unstable in all he does" (Jas. 1:2-8).

We must develop our faith through participation in the Body of Christ. Fear begets fear but faith also begets faith. If you want to be fearful, associate with people who are fearful. If you want to be pessimistic, associate with people who are pessimistic. But if you want to learn to trust God, associate with people who trust God. Observe their lives and you will draw strength from them.

This is a secret in developing divine perspective on life. I've experienced this in my own spiritual experience the last several years, particularly as I have participated in the body life of my church. True, the Word of God is basic in producing faith and trust in God. But learning what God says can easily become abstract truth that doesn't really affect our attitudes and behavior. The greatest impact in my own life of faith comes to me when I see God's truth fleshed out in the lives of other Christians. When I observe other Christians learning from their past mistakes, when I see brothers and sisters in Christ applying God's Word in their own lives, when I see fellow believers praying in faith and receiving answers to prayer—it's then I sense my own faith growing and developing. It's then my own spiritual perspectives are broadened and deepened. It's then that my own personal Christianity takes on new meaning and hope.

For example, almost every weekend for several years I have been involved in four two-and-one-half-hour services. The first hour I teach the Word but in the second hour I participate in the life of the body. In our church we call it fellowship and sharing. Some call it a "body life" service.

Lots of people, particularly pastors, have asked me how I could handle this responsibility physically and emotionally. The answer is quite simple: I am buoyed up spiritually through observing what God is doing in the lives of other members of the Body of Christ. And when I see what God is doing in the lives of other believers, it strengthens my faith. It encourages me to trust God personally. I see Christianity at work.

This should not be surprising. The Word of God teaches that we all need to learn the Word of God *and* have dynamic and vital relational experiences with each other in order to grow spiritually. In the words of Paul, "From him [Christ] the whole body, joined and held together by every supporting ligament, grows and builds itself up in love, as each part does its work" (Eph. 4:16).

A PERSONAL PROJECT

What are you doing to develop a divine perspective in your Christian life? In what areas are you strong? In what areas are you negligent? What are you going to do to be more obedient in carrying out God's will for your life?

The following evaluation will help you set some new goals:

1. I am learning from my past mistakes
   ☐ *seldom* ☐ *sometimes* ☐ *most of the time;*
2. I am seeking God's will:
   through learning His Word
   ☐ *seldom* ☐ *sometimes* ☐ *most of the time;*
   through regular private reading and study
   ☐ *seldom* ☐ *sometimes* ☐ *most of the time;*
   through regular exposure to public teaching of the Word
   ☐ *seldom* ☐ *sometimes* ☐ *most of the time;*

94

3. I am regularly participating in the life of the body in my church and entering into the following experiences with other Christians:

identifying the needs of others
☐ *seldom* ☐ *sometimes* ☐ *most of the time;*

praying for the needs of others
☐ *seldom* ☐ *sometimes* ☐ *most of the time;*

encouraging others
☐ *seldom* ☐ *sometimes* ☐ *most of the time;*

honoring others
☐ *seldom* ☐ *sometimes* ☐ *most of the time;*

greeting and welcoming others
☐ *seldom* ☐ *sometimes* ☐ *most of the time;*

serving others
☐ *seldom* ☐ *sometimes* ☐ *most of the time;*

bearing the burdens of others
☐ *seldom* ☐ *sometimes* ☐ *most of the time;*

sharing my concern and consecrated interest in others with my presence
☐ *seldom* ☐ *sometimes* ☐ *most of the time.*

A MAN WHO LOVED HIS ENEMY

1 Samuel 24:1-22; 26:1-25

There are two stories in the life of David that demonstrate dramatically his sensitivity toward both God and man. Both incidents involved encounters with Saul and both provided David with unusual opportunities to take Saul's life. But in each instance David did what was right, even though he faced unusual temptation. With his actions he showed love to the man who hated him.

DAVID'S FIRST OPPORTUNITY TO TAKE SAUL'S LIFE (1 Sam. 24:1-22)

David miraculously continued to escape Saul's death traps. On one occasion he was betrayed by the Ziphites, enabling Saul and his army to surround David and his small band of men (23:26). Humanly speaking, there was no way of escape. But just as it seemed that it was all over for David, the Philistines invaded Israel and

Saul had to give up his attack in order to pursue his larger interests. Once again we see God's sovereign protection of David.

The Setting

What happened next between Saul and David is ironic. David and his little band took refuge "in the strongholds of Engedi" a place designated as the "rocks of the wild goats." Here were numerous caverns and caves, one being so large that it is reported that it once sheltered 30,000 people from a terrible storm. Scholars believe this was the cave David used as a hiding place from Saul.

Following his most recent battle with the Philistines, Saul once again discovered David's general location. And once again, he pursued David, taking 3,000 of his best warriors with him.

While searching through the area, Saul himself took refuge from the hot sun in the very cave David and his men were hiding. Lurking in the shadows in the inner recesses of the cave, they were invisible to Saul. The darkness of the cave contrasted with the bright sunlight that permeated the wilderness of Engedi and made it very difficult for Saul to detect the presence of anyone.

David's men were overjoyed and understandably so. From their perspective here was David's golden opportunity. In fact, they interpreted the situation as the Lord's doing. Thus they said to David, "Behold, this is the day of which the Lord said to you, 'Behold; I am about to give your enemy into your hand, and you shall do to him as it seems good to you'" (24:4).

No doubt these men were paraphrasing some of David's psalms. Perhaps they remembered their previous experience in the cave of Adullam where David had penned Psalm 34. Had he not written, "The face of the Lord is against evildoers, to cut off the memory of them from the earth" (Ps. 34:16)? It is not surprising that they saw in their present cave experience, the grand opportunity to help the Lord eliminate David's greatest foe.

David's Attitudes and Actions

From a human perspective it all seemed logical. In these dark moments, David must have reflected on the times Saul had tried to pin him to the wall with his spear; the times Saul had sent him into battle with the Philistines hoping he would be killed; the many times Saul had nearly captured him with his well-trained army. What an opportunity to avenge himself! In fact, David seemingly was initially enamored with what appeared to be an opportunity from the Lord to take Saul's life.

To understand what actually transpired, we have to read between the lines of Scripture. Eventually Saul fell asleep in the coolness of the cave. While he dozed, David "arose and cut off the edge of Saul's robe secretly." But immediately, his "conscience bothered him" (24:4,5).

The question is *why*. There must have been something in David's heart—something about his motives— that troubled him regarding what appears to be a rather harmless act. Could it be that this was a selfish maneuver to symbolically demonstrate to his men that he was going to be the king of Israel? Was he going to use this to taunt Saul as his men captured him and took his life? Whatever David's motive, cutting off a piece of the king's robe seems to have been a preliminary step to taking Saul's life. Consequently, David's sensitive and well-informed conscience wouldn't let him pursue his scheme any further. He quickly acknowledged his error to his men and persuaded them not to harm Saul.

While sitting in the darkness waiting for Saul to leave the cave, David gained a proper perspective on the situation and decided to use the opportunity to achieve some goals God would definitely approve of. Consequently, when Saul awakened and left the cave, David followed him and called after him. With humility and deep respect for the king of Israel, he pleaded with Saul, demonstrating with the piece of Saul's robe that he was not trying to kill him. If he were, he would have taken the opportunity in the cave.

Saul's Reactions and Response

Saul's heart was temporarily troubled by David's actions. He knew his life had been spared. There was no way he could misconstrue the facts. Looking at his robe and the missing piece, he knew that David with one stroke could have severed his head from his body. He was humbled. He wept before David and confessed his wickedness. He acknowledged that God had delivered him into David's hands, and yet David had not killed him.

Saul was overwhelmed with David's actions. "If a man finds his enemy, will he let him go away safely?" queried Saul. "May the Lord therefore reward you with good in return for what you have done to me this day" (24:19).

As far as we know, Saul confessed for the first time publicly that he knew David was going to be the king of Israel. He only pleaded that David would spare his life and his descendants and relatives (24:20,21).

David, of course, promised he would not harm Saul's household. But he knew his time was not yet. Saul's repentance was not total. Nor had it been proven. If Saul were totally sincere at this point, he would have no doubt turned over his royal robe that day and anointed David king in his place. Rather he turned and went back to his throne and David and his men went on to find another place where they could live in safety. The true test was still ahead. Would the king suddenly change his attitudes toward David and pursue him once again as he had done so many times before? The answer, of course, is yes, and when it happened, the events paralleled quite closely this first opportunity to take Saul's life.

DAVID'S SECOND OPPORTUNITY TO TAKE SAUL'S LIFE (1 Sam. 26:1-25)

Anyone reading the story of David's life and his association with King Saul for the very first time could easily predict what was going to happen next.

The Setting

Saul reverted to his old patterns of behavior, just as he had done so many times before. Jealousy once again took over. His hatred for David possessed him and he went on another rampage, trying to find David and kill him.

As before, the Ziphites, seeking to gain some prestige and position with the king, fed information to Saul regarding David's whereabouts. And once again, Saul put together an army of 3,000 choice men and began to search for David in the wilderness of Ziph.

David's Attitudes and Actions

Events in this story are similar to the first, but yet distinctive. One night while Saul and his army were asleep, David and one of his men, Abishai, crept into the enemy camp. The Lord had caused a deep sleep to come upon Saul and his total company of soldiers. Even Abner, Saul's chief bodyguard was fast asleep.

Abishai, recognizing immediately another golden opportunity to once and for all deal with Saul, begged David to let him kill the king. But once again David protected Saul. Taking the king's spear and a jug of water that were beside his head, they left the camp. They descended the valley and climbed up on another mountain. From there David called—not to Saul—to Abner, chiding him for allowing the king to go unattended and unprotected.

David's speech is classic. He taught Saul a lesson even though he was directing his words at Abner. "Are you not a man?" he called. "And who is like you in Israel? Why then have you not guarded your lord the king? For one of the people came to destroy the king your lord. This thing that you have done is not good. As the Lord lives, all of you must surely die, because you did not guard your lord, the Lord's anointed. And now, see where the king's spear is, and the jug of water that was at his head" (26:15,16).

David's point is obvious. David himself had served as a better bodyguard to Saul than Abner. Furthermore, David was saying that someone so careless should die. Saul, of course, got the point. David was implying that it was totally irrational for Saul to seek his life when those who were on Saul's side were not as concerned for his life as David was.

Saul's Reactions and Response

Once again Saul realized that he was falsely judging David. He invited David to come with him, promising never to attempt to take his life again. David, however, could no longer trust the king. He returned Saul's spear but turned and went on his way. David knew that he could never be totally safe in Saul's presence, but he also knew he had conveyed to the king his own pure motives. His conscience was clear, though he would have to live as a fugitive until the Lord Himself removed Saul.

TWENTIETH-CENTURY LESSONS

How David handled these two situations yields some dynamic lessons for twentieth-century Christians who may be facing enemies in their own lives.

David recognized that Saul was anointed by God. He was no ordinary enemy. Brothers and sisters in Christ who may be troubling us in some way are not ordinary enemies either. They may be out to hurt us, their motives may be selfish, they may be vindictive toward us, but this does not entitle the Christian to return evil for evil to another Christian. In fact, a Christian is not to return evil to anyone. Jesus Himself set a very high standard when He said, "You have heard that it was said, 'Love your neighbor and hate your enemy.' But I tell you, Love your enemies and pray for those who persecute you, that you may be sons of your Father in heaven. He causes his sun to rise on the evil and the good, and sends rain on the righteous and unrighteous. If you love those who love you, what reward will you get? Are not even the tax collectors doing that? And if you greet only your brothers, what are you doing more than others? Do not even pagans do that? Be perfect, therefore, as your heavenly Father is perfect" (Matt. 5:43-48).

David developed a sensitive conscience that was in tune with God's will. A Christian's conscience is a very important part of his total being. And it is very important that it be in tune with the Word of God. Some people develop an oversensitive conscience, one that is tuned to man's will rather than God's. For example, I used to feel guilty about things for which I shouldn't have felt guilty. This was because my conscience was related to man-made rules and regulations for spirituality rather than God's rules.

On the other hand, some develop an insensitive conscience that is out of harmony with God's will. Paul refers to people like these when he states that their "consciences have been seared as with a hot iron" (1 Tim. 4:2).

David's conscience was sensitive, but not oversensitive. He knew what was right and what was wrong because of his personal relationship with God. And in this case he knew it would be wrong to take Saul's life, even though his men felt he had a perfect right to do so.

Though David was tempted to return evil for evil, he checked his behavior before he reached the point of no return. Every Christian is tempted to do wrong, especially when someone treats him badly. Under these circumstances, most of us initially react emotionally and defensively and move in the direction of doing wrong before we gain a proper spiritual perspective. The important lesson from David's life is that we check ourselves before we do something we cannot correct without serious consequences.

At this point some Christians are very vulnerable. They find it easy to rationalize. Once they move in the direction of being vindictive, they decide they may as well go all the way. Not so with David. Even under social pressure he acknowledged his improper motives and turned away from doing wrong.

David did not succumb to social pressure. In both instances David was encouraged by others to vindicate himself by taking Saul's life (see 1 Sam. 24:4; 26:8). It would have been easy for him to rationalize, "After all, others believe it is the right thing to do." Furthermore, Saul had tried to take David's life many times. Even so, David knew what was right. And in this situation he changed the crowd; he didn't allow the crowd to change him.

David defended himself against Saul, but he did so with humility and respect. Some Christians believe they have no rights. This is not true. David had a perfect right to defend himself. But he did so in a proper way. He confronted Saul with the facts. He demonstrated his loyalty to the king. He shared his inner feelings of frustration and stress. He pleaded with Saul to understand.

The apostle Paul is an outstanding New Testament example of a Christian who defends himself. When he was wronged, particularly by Christians, he set the record straight firmly, but in love.

David acknowledged that God is ultimately responsible to inflict punishment on those whose hearts are hardened toward Him. In both situations David made his point very clear. During the first encounter with Saul, David said, "May the Lord judge between you and me, and may the Lord avenge me on you; but my hand shall not be against you . . . . The Lord therefore be judge and decide between you and me; and may He see and plead my cause, and deliver me from your hand" (1 Sam. 24:12,15).

During the second encounter with Saul, David had also said to Abishai, who wanted to take Saul's life, "As the Lord lives, surely the Lord will strike him, or his day will come that he dies, or he will go down into battle and perish" (1 Sam. 26:10).

Paul in the New Testament summarized God's will for Christians in matters like this when he wrote to the Romans: "Do not repay anyone evil for evil. Be careful to do what is right in the sight of everybody. If it is possible, as far as it depends on you, live at peace with everyone. Do not take revenge, my friends, but leave room for God's wrath, for it is written: 'It is mine to avenge, I will repay,' says the Lord. On the contrary: 'If your enemy is hungry, feed him; if he is thirsty, give him something to drink. In doing this, you will heap burning coals on his head.' Do not be overcome by evil, but overcome evil with good" (Rom. 12:17-21).

Though David in these two instances followed God's principles in dealing with Saul, he realized that he could never totally trust the king again. This is clear from David's behavior. And understandably so. When Saul invited David to come and be in his presence following the second encounter, David's reply was kind but clear cut. He had made his point with Saul—he did not return evil for evil—but he in no way would entrust his life to the king. Consequently, "David went on his way, and Saul returned to his place" (1 Sam. 26:25).

Though Christians are to forgive, though they are to do everything they can to re-establish trust, though they are to go the extra mile even with their enemies—there are times in some relationships when it is no longer possible to trust another person totally. Saul again and again demonstrated his untrustworthiness and un-predictable behavior. David knew he could never have total confidence in him again. Thus David said, as he concluded the conversation from his perspective, "Now behold, as your life was highly valued in my sight this day, so may my life be highly valued in the sight of the Lord, and may He deliver me from all distress" (1 Sam. 26:24). In other words David was saying at no time would he ever take Saul's life. He had demonstrated that beyond doubt. However, the only one who could protect his life from Saul was the Lord. Never again would he trust the king.

Note: Remember that it is easy to rationalize that another person cannot be trusted. Before you ever take this course of action, identify with David's numerous attempts to trust Saul before he took this final course of action.

A PERSONAL PROJECT
All of us have people in our lives who try to hurt us. Identify one of those individuals and use David's exam-

ple to evaluate your own attitudes and actions:

1. I have done all I can to approach this person on a spiritual basis, realizing they too are made in the image of God.

2. In my relationships with this person, my conscience is tuned to the *will* and *Word* of God, not to what *I* want to do to the person.

3. When I am tempted to return evil for evil to this person, I am able to check my behavior before I've done something irreversible and damaging to my own personal testimony.

4. I do not go along with the crowd in my attitudes and actions toward this unlovable person.

5. I defend myself when I'm wronged, but I do so with humility and respect.

6. My attitudes and actions toward this person reflect the fact that I believe that God will ultimately make things right—even if I cannot.

7. Recognizing that some people will never be trustworthy, I have not allowed mistrust to become a part of my behavior prematurely. In other words, I've done all I can possibly do to correct the situation. Furthermore, I have not allowed a bad experience with one or several people to cause me to mistrust people in general.

10

A MAN WHO SOUGHT REVENGE

1 Samuel 25

In many ways the story of David is a story of contrasts, not only in his relationship with Saul but in relationship to himself. Though he was evidently a man small in stature, he was known in the kingdom for his largeness of heart, his great love for God and his unique compassion for mankind. Though he was never technically trained in the arts and sciences, he became the greatest poet and musician in the Old Testament. Though he was uninitiated in normal battle techniques, he became a hero when he slew Goliath and led the army of Israel into numerous victories over the Philistines. Though he was a son of a lowly farmer in Israel, his best friend Jonathan was a prince and the son of a king. Though a man of great faith, he at times was paralyzed with fear. And as we have observed in our last chapter he demonstrated great patience and love toward his enemy Saul when he had two unique opportunities to take his life.

In our present study we will see that David became angry and resentful when his kindness toward a man named Nabal was rejected. This final observation, of course, points to a contrast in his personality that is frequently seen in great Christians: though David was a man after God's own heart, he was still a human being and sometimes he failed the Lord miserably. More specifically, the contrast we observe in this event in David's life is that he moved from a situation where he demonstrated great patience and love toward King Saul, who consistently was trying to take his life. Then under a much less stressful situation, David allowed himself to become very angry and resentful when he was rejected by a rich fool.

THE STORY OF A FOOL (1 Sam. 25:1-42)

Following Samuel's death David and his men headed south to the wilderness of Paran, a sparsely populated area. In fact, it was in this part of the country that the children of Israel wandered for many years before entering the land of Canaan. For a time, at least, David felt safe from his enemy, King Saul. But it was here that David encountered a more subtle enemy, a man whose selfish and greedy behavior he wasn't mentally, emotionally, or spiritually prepared to handle. This man's name was Nabal, which literally means "fool." And fool he was! Nabal could very well have been a mental image in Jesus' mind when He told the parable of the rich man as recorded by Luke in his Gospel (see Luke 12:13-21).

Though the story of Nabal in itself forms the basis for some tremendous lessons for Christians and non-Christians alike, I'm more interested in David's reactions to this man's foolish and selfish behavior.

The Rich Man

By all standards Nabal *was* a rich man. "He had three thousand sheep and a thousand goats" (25:2). And one of his greatest assets was a beautiful and intelligent wife named Abigail who, unlike her husband, was a very sensitive and unselfish person.

For many days David's men had lived in the area where Nabal's shepherds grazed his sheep. In fact, they had often protected these men and their animals from harm and danger. One of Nabal's own shepherds stated it well: "The men were very good to us, and we were not insulted, nor did we miss anything as long as we went about with them, while we were in the fields. They were a wall to us both by night and by day, all the time we were with them tending the sheep" (25:15,16).

The time came when Nabal was ready to cash in on his investments. For most people this was a season of liberality and good will, a time to share one's blessings with others. Consequently, David sent 10 of his men to talk with Nabal about his army's need for food and clothing. After all, they had treated him well, helping to guard his flocks. It seemed only logical and reasonable to make this request in view of all that David had done for him.

David's Message

"Go up to Carmel," said David, "visit Nabal and greet him in *my name*; and thus you shall say, 'Have a long life, peace be to you, and peace be to your house, and peace be to all that you have" (25:5,6).

Nabal's response devastated David's ego. When the young men asked for food, they and David were totally unprepared for Nabal's response. He hurled the greatest insult at David any man could ever give another: "Who is David? And who is the son of Jesse?" he queried. "There are many servants today who are each breaking away from his master. Shall I then take my bread and my water and my meat that I have slaughtered for my shearers, and give it to men whose origin I do not know?" (25:10,11).

To refuse to share his produce was insult enough in the light of what David had done for him. But to actually deny any knowledge of who David was and to classify him as a runaway slave was indeed a horrible put-down that infuriated the future king of Israel. David's anger reached fever pitch. He grabbed his sword and ordered 400 men to do the same. He vowed he would kill every man associated with Nabal, which no doubt included Nabal himself.

Abigail's Intercession

Fortunately, one of Nabal's servants was perceptive enough to predict what was going to happen when he observed the ill-treatment Nabal gave David's men. Knowing that Abigail, Nabal's wife, would understand clearly what was about to transpire, the servant lost no time finding her and telling her the whole story. And understand she did! Hurriedly, and without consulting her husband, she prepared an abundance of food and went out to meet David. Humbling herself at his feet, she took the blame for her husband's irresponsible actions and begged for mercy.

David's heart was touched and humbled by this woman's behavior. He immediately recognized God's hand in what was happening. "Blessed be the Lord God of Israel," David said, "who sent you this day to meet me, and blessed be your discernment, and blessed be you, who have kept me this day from bloodshed, and from avenging myself by my own hand" (25:32,33).

David received Abigail's gift of food and sent her on her way in peace. The end of the story, however, in some respects is ironical. When Abigail returned home she discovered that Nabal had over-celebrated on this festive occasion. Rejoicing in his good fortune, he became so drunk with wine that he was incapable of carrying on an intelligent conversation. But in the morning when he was sober, Abigail told him what she had done. The story so gripped Nabal emotionally (there was either anger or fear or both) that he experienced a stroke. The text says that "his heart died within him so that he became as a stone" (25:37). He never recovered. Ten days later he died. In fact in this case, the Lord judged Nabal for his wickedness and took his life (see 25:38).

The last scene in this dramatic story is even more ironical. When David heard of Nabal's death, he sent a proposal to Abigail to become his wife. She accepted. Nabal not only lost his life but his wife was married to the man he refused to help, whom he denied even knowing.

TWENTIETH-CENTURY LESSONS
Many valuable lessons emerge from this twenty-fifth chapter.

Before this event David had just experienced a great victory in the area of patience and love toward his enemy. King Saul had persistently tried to kill him, and, in a secluded cave where Saul lay sleeping, David could have snuffed out his life with a single thrust of his spear. This was his opportunity. Even when David was ministering to Saul in his periods of depression, the king had tried to pin him to the wall with his own spear. Why not even the score? But David didn't. He loved his enemy who had again and again returned evil for good.

Comparatively speaking, Nabal's insults and humili-

111

ating comments were minor. Anyone would expect this kind of behavior from a fool. But David lost control of himself and almost committed mass murder.

As a twentieth-century Christian, have you ever passed the big test in your life and then failed the little one? Be careful. We are most vulnerable when we are coming off our most successful experiences in the Christian life. Paul warned, "Let him who thinks he stands take heed lest he fall" (1 Cor. 10:12, *NASB*).

David's uncontrolled anger related more to an attack on his self-image than on his life. Saul tried to kill David many times. By contrast Nabal simply rejected him and put him down. With biting sarcasm he denied he even knew who David was, a low blow indeed!

All of us are most vulnerable to anger when we are personally attacked or put down. Often we can handle physical threat much better than psychological threat. Let someone puncture our ego, attack our self-image and tear down our public reputation, then we are in danger of losing control of our emotions. This is what happened to David.

David made his decision to act while in an angry state of mind. Anyone in David's position would no doubt have experienced angry feelings. He was a human being like all of us. This kind of rejection is difficult to handle emotionally. David's mistake, however, was to make a decision and to act on that decision while he was in an angry mood.

This is a tendency in all human beings, even Christians. Consequently, Paul warned the Ephesian Christians: "In your anger do not sin: Do not let the sun go down while you are still angry, and do not give the devil a foothold" (Eph. 4:26,27).

Here Paul acknowledged that all anger is not sin. It

becomes sin, however, when we act in improper ways. This was David's mistake and if it were not for the grace of God he would have committed a serious crime against humanity.

David allowed himself to be quick-tempered. David flew off the handle, to use a common expression of yesteryear. Stated in more contemporary fashion, he lost his cool.

This kind of quick-temperedness is a mark of immaturity in the Christian life. In his pastoral epistles to Timothy and Titus, Paul warned them not to appoint men to leadership in the church who have this problem. Quoting Paul specifically, he said, "Since an overseer is entrusted with God's work, he must be blameless—not overbearing, not *quick-tempered* . . . not violent" (Titus 1:7).

David failed the test in this area of his life on this particular occasion. All of us periodically have this same problem even as spiritual leaders. Our goal should be to eliminate this behavior from our life-style, to learn to control our temper and, above all, to correct a situation when it happens, asking forgiveness and making amends when we have hurt someone in the process.

David took matters into his own hands and tried to take revenge. David's pride was definitely hurt. He was out to avenge himself. He even generalized his anger to include innocent people. Though one man was the source of his hurt and his anger, David was going to wipe out all of Nabal's menservants.

Fortunately, Abigail intervened. And David was eternally grateful. By his own confession he realized he had sought revenge, and he knew it would have been a terrible sin.

In David's case God brought judgment upon Nabal.

Though all such incidents cannot be classified as God's specific act of wrath, there will come a day when God will settle all accounts of wrongdoing. Apart from crime that should be cared for and settled by the law courts, we are not to try to avenge ourselves in the area of personal injuries. If we cannot settle such problems through mature dialogue and communication, we must leave them to God. It is His prerogative to eventually settle these matters (see Rom. 12:17-21).

A PERSONAL PROJECT

In the following suggestions for handling anger in yourself and others, put a plus mark (+) by those suggestions where you feel you are quite successful. Put a minus (−) where you feel you need improvement. Then pray asking God to help you change your approach to specific problems.

How to Handle Anger in Yourself

1. Try not to be caught off guard. We are often the most vulnerable when we feel we've got it together.

2. Remember that anger often relates significantly to our self-image. It is easier to handle physical threats than psychological threats. Insecurity breeds quick-temperedness.

3. Don't make significant decisions and take specific actions when you are angry. Wait until you have gained perspective and control. It is often helpful to talk the problem out with a third person who is objective.

4. Deal with quick-temperedness. Reprogram your mind not to respond with threats and insecure reactions. Try to perceive every difficult situation as a learning experience rather than a personal attack.

5. Never try to get even or to take vengeance on someone who has hurt you. This does not mean you shouldn't communicate directly attempting to straight-

en out the matter, but try to do so honestly, openly and in a state of emotional control—and with the other person's interest at heart.

How to Handle Anger in Others

1. Do not counter anger with anger. Remember that "A gentle answer turns away wrath, but a harsh word stirs up anger" (Prov. 15:1).

2. Try to understand the source of the anger. Realize that most people lose control because of a high threat level or because of a series of events that have created a great deal of frustration and anxiety. You may be observing the straw that broke the camel's back. Try to put the person at ease, accepting his feelings. Remember that, "Pleasant words are a honeycomb, sweet to the soul and healing to the bones" (Prov. 16:24).

3. Listen to the person before responding. Try to get a perspective on the person's feelings—even if they are directed at you. Remember too that frequently people who are angry use others as scapegoats. Even though they may be attacking you, you may not be the main source of frustration. Remember also these words: "Like apples of gold in settings of silver is a word spoken in *right* circumstances" (Prov. 25:11).

11

DAVID
LOSES
PERSPECTIVE

1 Samuel 27:1—28:2; 29:1-4; 30:1-20

Have you ever faced a serious conflict in your life that led you to make a decision that eventually left you in a worse state than before? At first, your decision seemed to be the right thing to do. Perhaps you felt it was the only thing to do—even though down deep you knew what you were doing was contrary to God's will. In fact, somewhat surprising to you, things went a lot better after you made the decision. You felt better! You had more prestige! You even made more money! And you made more friends! Some of your enemies even seemed to be at peace with you. After all, you reasoned, how could God be displeased with my new life-style since I have all of these benefits and blessings as a result of the decision?

116

In retrospect, of course, you now understand that you were rationalizing. In fact, it's hard to believe you made such a foolish decision. But you did! And what refocused your thinking was a whole new set of problems that eventually emerged. Problems so complex there was nowhere to turn but back to God! And turn you did. And in God's love and grace He welcomed you back home, back where you belong, and back into His perfect will.

In many respects this basic experience was David's experience. And in the process he learned some painful lessons. Let's look at the dynamics involved. There are some tremendous lessons for us too!

DAVID'S RESPONSE TO REJECTION (1 Sam. 27:1-3)

David reached a new low point in his emotional and spiritual life as a result of a series of encounters with Saul. Again and again he was threatened and rejected by the king of Israel. He was betrayed by those who were supposed to be his friends. He and his little band of men were forced to travel hither and yon, looking for a place to hide from his enemies. When he experienced two unusual opportunities to take Saul's life (see 1 Sam. 24; 26) he turned the other cheek and spared the king of Israel.

David apparently began to experience deep feelings of isolation and rejection from God. From our vantage point of course we can see clearly that God was not rejecting David nor forsaking him. However, in the midst of his wilderness wanderings, David lost perspective on God's protective hand. Several of his psalms, which many believe were written during this time, reflect these feelings. "Why dost Thou stand afar off, O Lord? Why dost Thou hide Thyself in times of trouble?" he wrote in Psalm 10:1. And in Psalm 13, verses 1 and 2 he poured out his soul to God, reflecting these deep feelings of rejection: "How long, O Lord? Wilt Thou forget me forever? How long wilt Thou hide Thy face from me? How long shall I take counsel in my soul, having sorrow in my heart all the day? How long will my enemy be exalted over me?"

Perhaps his deepest expression of grief and anxiety is recorded in Psalm 22: "My God, my God, why hast Thou forsaken me?" (Ps. 22:1).

He Felt Sorry for Himself

Like most of us enmeshed in this kind of predicament, David felt sorry for himself. Self-pity began to dominate his total being. After all, he had turned the other cheek. He had gone the extra mile. He had just spared his archenemy, the king of Israel. Had he not been loyal and faithful both to his king on earth and to his King in heaven? Why weren't things going better? A logical question indeed!

David's feelings are understandable. But unfortunately his emotional state of self-pity led him to take actions that were definitely out of God's will. After thinking through the situation he decided he'd once again take matters into his own hands and resolve the problem. Without consulting God he made the decision to leave the land of Israel and travel into enemy territory seeking asylum. Thus we read: "Then David said to himself, 'Now I will perish one day by the hand of Saul. There is nothing better for me than to escape into the land of the Philistines. Saul then will despair of searching for me any more in all the territory of Israel, and I will escape from his hand' " (27:1).

He Became Confused

David's thinking at this moment in his life reflects confusion from several perspectives.

First, to conclude that Saul was going to eventually

kill him was in direct contradiction to what God had promised. By direct revelation God had made it very clear that David would be the next king of Israel (see 16:1). However, in the midst of his depression and feelings of rejection David either forgot God's Word or lost faith in what God had said. If he was like many of us (and he was), at this moment in his life he probably couldn't even remember the promise or the many times God had supernaturally protected him from Saul's evil intentions.

Second, to conclude that there would be "nothing better for me than to escape into the land of the Philistines" was definitely in opposition to the will of God. On numerous occasions the Lord had warned Israel never to develop deep relationships with pagan people (and as we'll see this was David's intention in the land of the Philistines), knowing full well that the Israelites would imbibe their life-style, be influenced by their value system and eventually worship their false gods. I'm confident David knew in his heart that he was violating God's commandments and that he was subjecting his family and hundreds of other families to a pagan and degenerate environment.

This leads us to a very important observation that is a clue in understanding David's thinking and behavior at this time in his life. Note that he said: "There is nothing better for *me* than to escape into the land of the Philistines." David was first and foremost thinking of himself—of his own anxieties, of his own problems, of his own fears and feelings of rejection. In the midst of this emotional misery, selfishness dominated his being. His family and friends were secondary. Rationalization and self-preservation took over.

THE RESULTS OF DAVID'S ACTIONS (1 Sam. 27:4-7)

The most subtle part of being out of God's will is often

119

what surfaces as positive results, especially involving emotional rewards. This clearly happened in David's life.

Saul Quit the Chase

The pressure was off. Saul no longer tried to kill David. When the king discovered that "David had fled to Gath . . . he no longer searched for him" (27:4). For the first time in months and even in years David felt free from the pressures of pursuit.

David Felt Accepted

Whatever the dynamics, David found acceptance at Gath, something he didn't find in the land of Israel. And also of significance, this acceptance was by a king! The king of Gath, who had rejected him before when he feigned insanity (see 21:10,15), now welcomed him.

How did David ingratiate himself with Achish? Think of the fantastic tale of faithful commitment to Saul that David could relate. And think too how this might have impressed Achish. Perhaps David's story went something like this:

King Achish, I spent many years serving Saul. I was his faithful armor-bearer. I won many of his battles. I even slew your giant Goliath—you'll remember that, Sir. I was just a young boy. But, Sir, Saul has never appreciated my loyalty. In fact, as you know, he has tried to take my life many times.

I have never been disloyal to King Saul, Sir. I even had two very recent opportunities to kill him. One was in a cave. He was asleep. I could have killed him with one blow. But I didn't. I spared his life. I consider him the Lord's anointed.

Another opportunity came one night when

120

Saul was sound asleep in the center of his camp. He was looking for me, trying to kill me. I slipped into the midst of the camp and stood beside him. There he was sound asleep. Again one blow would have killed him. But I didn't, Sir. I only took his spear and water bottle and left. Later I called to him trying to demonstrate that I was not trying to take his life. Though Saul confessed his own hatred toward me and promised me he would not hurt me, I could never trust him again. I have only experienced repeated rejection from him. If it please you, Sir, please provide me with a place of safety and I'll serve you rather than Saul. You can trust me.

It only stands to reason that David would have related these facts to Achish. And, if he believed David at all, the king would certainly be impressed. In fact, this information would definitely appeal to his ego. How ironic to have at his disposal Saul's faithful servant-turned-traitor. What more could a king want in order to give him an inside track in discovering the secret of Israel's many victories over the Philistines? Achish no doubt realized, too, that Israel's God was with David. Perhaps to befriend David would also give him an inside track to the God of Israel. After all, God was the Israelites' guarantee to victory, a very obvious fact to the enemies of the Israelites. It is only logical that a pagan king, who would worship any god, would embrace another one in order to reach his goals.

The People Found a Home

David and his band of followers were given a secure place to live, first in the royal city and eventually in their own city. Something happened between David and Achish that caused this enemy of Israel to trust David and give him a place of refuge. Both of these men had one thing in common—an enemy named Saul. Achish knew full well of Saul's repeated attempts on David's life and obviously, this helped David establish credibility with the Philistine king.

Realize of course that David's relationship with Achish developed one step at a time. The king's first act of kindness was to allow David and his men and their families to live in the royal city. Eventually David must have convinced Achish he was his friend. For, in time, he approached the king and asked a rather large favor, indicating unusual rapport: "Then David said to Achish, 'If now I have found favor in your sight, let them give me a place in one of the cities in the country, that I may live there; for why should your servant live in the royal city with you?' " (27:5).

Note David's tact with Achish. His appeal was based on unworthiness to live in the same city with the king. His approach worked. The king's answer was astonishing, reflecting even greater credibility and trust: "So Achish gave him Ziklag that day," an abandoned city which served as an ideal place for David's men and their families (27:6). It was formerly a city inhabited by Israel and subsequently captured by the Philistines.

Initially then, David's escape into the land of the Philistines resulted in very positive benefits. He was free from Saul's attempts on his life; he felt an acceptance by the king; and he was given a place to live. But there is yet another factor that would be interpreted very positively by David. The author of 1 Chronicles records that when the valiant warriors in Saul's army heard of David's acceptance by the King of Gath and how he had received the city of Ziklag as a gift from the king, many deserted Saul and joined David. We read, "For day by day men came to David to help him, until there was a great army like the army of God" (1 Chron. 12:22).

David's faithful 600 soon turned into thousands. You can imagine how this phenomenon bolstered David's self-image and reassured him that he had indeed made the right decision. How easy it would have been for him to rationalize that this was all in God's plan to make him the next king.

DAVID'S TROUBLES START
(1 Sam. 27:8—28:2; 29:1-4; 30:1-20)

As always when a man of God walks out of the will of God, trouble lies ahead. It may come suddenly or gradually, but eventually it comes and multiplies rapidly. How true this was in David's experience.

The People Needed Food

One of David's first problems was of providing food for his growing company of followers. This led to a cruel maneuver. He and his men invaded the Geshurites, the Gerzites and the Amalekites, most of whom were herdsmen (see 27:8). Though these people were enemies of Israel they had not provoked this battle. God gave no specific order for this particular attack, as He had in years gone by, neither did He give David permission to take any of their herds, their flocks, and their clothing (see 27:9).

This act led to another problem: These people were evidently friendly with the Philistines; what would Achish say when he heard? David had two alternatives. He could acknowledge what he had done and seek forgiveness from the king, or he could keep Achish from finding out the facts. He chose the latter and, in order to keep Achish from hearing about it, David took the life of every individual in the land—including women and children, an act that would later haunt him. "Dead men tell no tales" was David's rationale (see 27:9,11).

But this wrong action led to still another problem. He

could destroy the evidence of who it was he attacked but he could not hide the fact that he had raided a people. For he brought back a rather substantial booty including sheep, cattle, donkeys, camels, and clothing (see 27:9).

David Deceived Achish

Sure enough Achish asked, "Where have you made a raid today?" (27:10). Again David had a choice. He could acknowledge his unfortunate behavior, or tell a boldfaced lie. And, again he chose the latter. And lie he did! But with an additional motive. David reported that his attack was against Israel. Because there was no evidence who these people really were, and since David's army was returning from the same direction as the border of Israel, "Achish believed David, saying, 'He has surely made himself odious among his people Israel; therefore he will become my servant forever' " (27:12).

For David the plot was thickening. On the surface, he was gaining prestige in the eyes of the Philistine king. But in the eyes of God he was sinking deeper and deeper into the mire of sin and walking farther and farther out of the will of God. And his biggest problem still lay ahead, for sin pays rich dividends, even though they may accumulate for a period of time before the final payoff. But David did receive his "wages of sin," first gradually and then with a crushing force.

Caught in a Lie

David faced his first real dilemma when Achish decided to make war against Israel. By now David had established such credibility that the king planned for David to go into battle with him (see 28:1). David had no excuse. He could only nod an affirmative answer. You can imagine David's surprise when Achish answered that he was going to make him his personal bodyguard (see 28:2).

What was he to do? David certainly could not fight against his own people. But what were his alternatives now? To reveal all would have been virtual suicide, not only for himself but for his people. Any other excuse would appear superficial. He was too indebted to this man of the world to even attempt to back out. His only choice was to feign excitement about the projected battle and hope that God would intervene—the God he had been ignoring and whose laws he had been violating.

But once again God's grace became evident in David's life and from a most unexpected source. Achish's military leaders became suspicious of David and his men. They insisted that David's army not be allowed to join them in their fight against Israel lest they seize the opportunity to make an inside attack on the Philistines. What better way, they reasoned, could David gain merit in Saul's eyes (see 29:4)? Achish, though he disagreed, succumbed to the request. Once again David feigned interest in the battle, acting surprised and disappointed, but inwardly he was breathing a sigh of relief.

Little did David suspect what lay ahead in the way of surprise and remorse. When David's men returned to Ziklag, the city had been attacked by the Amalekites. The army had burned the city to the ground and taken captive all who were in the city—women, children and those men who had not joined David. David and his men did not know whether their loved ones were dead or alive. They probably thought of their own merciless raid earlier on a group of the very people who had retaliated.

Remorse and Rejection

Two things happened! First, there was a great sorrow among the men. They "lifted their voices and wept until there was no strength in them to weep" (30:4). The next event shook David so severely it brought him to his senses. Many of the men were so angry and depressed that they actually proposed stoning David (see 30:6).

At this point David reached his low point. Suddenly his life for the past months flashed before his eyes. Seeing himself as God saw him he reached up to the Lord for help, perhaps for the first time since he left the environment of Israel. "David strengthened himself in the Lord his God" (30:6). This was the beginning of restoration for David.

David's next move reflects the old David—the man after God's own heart. Immediately he communicated with the Lord, seeking His will and advice. Receiving permission from the Lord to pursue the Amalekites, he rescued every person alive and well, another evidence of God's grace (see 30:19). Had David received an "eye for an eye" and a "tooth for a tooth"—which he really deserved—he would have become a desperate man. David suffered for his mistakes but God restored him and he once again began walking with the Lord.

TWENTIETH-CENTURY LESSONS

David learned some very painful lessons through this experience in the land of the Philistines. Hopefully, we can learn lessons from David's life and avoid circumstances that cause pain. God is explicit in the Old Testament regarding His most respected servants because He wants us to learn from their mistakes. Thus Paul wrote to the Corinthians: "These things happened to them as examples and were written down as warnings for us, on whom the fulfillment of the ages has come" (1 Cor. 10:11).

Beware of the effects of self-pity, especially when its source is rejection. It can easily lead to very self-centered decisions that eventually are disastrous. This was David's problem. He felt rejected both by Saul and by

God. Consequently, he made his decision based on his own personal needs, without regard for others or God's will. It led to serious consequences.

As a Christian, beware of losing perspective on God's plan for your life. Attempt to think long-range. Remember, there will be periods of confusion and darkness in your life. Some of these periods God allows to test us; others come because we are in a sinful world. But in all of them God wants us to wait out the storm. His "grace is sufficient" and His "power is made perfect in weakness" (2 Cor. 12:9).

David lost perspective on God's will for his life. In the midst of his wilderness experience he forgot the promise of God and was unable to remember God's previous solutions.

Don't interpret blessings in your life as necessarily a sign of God's approval of your behavior. Some Christians make this mistake and justify making decisions that contradict God's revealed will. For example, I've heard people say to me, "But I *feel* so much better separated from my wife or husband." Or, "God must be pleased with what I'm doing; otherwise, why would I be making so much money."

Obviously, an unhappy relationship brings emotional relief when the cause of that stress is eliminated. This was true of David. He felt better when he was out from under Saul's persecution. But this did not mean he was in the will of God.

And regarding material blessings, remember God "causes his sun to rise on the evil and the good, and sends rain on the righteous and the unrighteous" (Matt. 5:45). David's mistake was that he evidently interpreted all of the blessings and acceptance he received in the land of the Philistines as a sign of God's blessing, not realizing that he was falling prey to the selfish needs and motives of a worldly king.

Don't take advantage of God's grace. God *does* love us and we are His children. He will never reject us or disown us. His love is infinite. Nothing "will be able to separate us from the love of God that is in Christ Jesus our Lord" (Rom. 8:39).

But God *will* discipline us (see Heb. 12:7-11). In most instances His discipline consists of allowing us to suffer the natural consequences of our sin, which may not be obvious immediately. But the problems will come, just as they did in David's life. And in the process, we not only hurt ourselves but we also hurt those closest to us.

If we understand God's grace, we'll never take advantage of it, we'll be taught by it. Paul wrote to Titus: "The grace of God that brings salvation has appeared to all men. It teaches us to say 'No' to ungodliness and worldly passions, and to live self-controlled, upright and godly lives in this present age, while we wait for the blessed hope—the glorious appearing of our great God and Savior, Jesus Christ, who gave himself for us to redeem us from all wickedness and to purify for himself a people that are his very own, eager to do what is good" (Titus 2:11-14).

It is never too late to turn back to God. Though we may have to reap what we have sown, God's grace and forgiveness are always available to all who call upon Him, whether Christian or non-Christian. At David's lowest point, when he had nowhere to turn, when his own self-centered strategies ultimately failed, he "strengthened himself in the Lord his God." He acknowledged his mistakes. He once again began to walk in God's ways. Don't let pride stand in your way. Remember that "everyone who calls on the name of the

Lord will be saved" (Rom. 10:13). Furthermore, "If we confess our sins, he is faithful and just and will forgive us our sins and purify us from all unrighteousness" (1 John 1:9). There's no sin too great for God to forgive.

A PERSONAL PROJECT

Use the following lessons from David's life as checkpoints in your own life. Which ones apply to you? Isolate your own area of need and decide today that you are going to refocus your life in that particular area and begin today to walk in the will of God.

1. I am prone to self-pity and selfish decisions that lead me out of the will of God.

2. I easily lose perspective on God's plan for my life which also leads to improper decisions.

3. I sometimes interpret blessings in my life as a sign of God's approval on my disobedience.

4. I tend to take advantage of God's grace in the way I live as a Christian.

5. I am at a low point in my life and I need to turn back to God.

12

DAVID'S GREATEST SIN

2 Samuel 11:1—12:23

Following David's disobedience in seeking refuge in the land of the Philistines and his eventual repentance and restoration, the next major event that affected his life dramatically was Saul's death on the battlefield on Mount Gilboa (see 1 Sam. 31). How thankful David must have been that God had supernaturally and sovereignly delivered him from having to participate in the very battle against Israel in which Saul and David's soul brother, Jonathan, were slain. Had he been party to the death of the Lord's anointed and to that of his best friend, he would never have forgiven himself. As it was, his sorrow and mourning for them reflected deep love, and also revealed the David whose heart could be so right toward both God and man (see 2 Sam. 1).

Following the death of Saul the events leading to David's kingship gradually unfolded. For seven and one-half years David served as king of Judah. Then he was anointed as ruler of all Israel.

These days of transition were generally good days for David. He walked with God and consulted Him. He demonstrated great wisdom and justice in Israel. He waited for God's timing in the matters before him. He experienced numerous victories over the enemies of Israel and eventually established Jerusalem as a capital city. Compared to the pagan kings who ruled around him, David stood out as one of the greatest spiritual leaders in Old Testament history.

But then it happened, nearly 20 years after he first occupied the throne. He committed one of the greatest sins of his life! A sin that was eventually forgiven but one that continued to pay its wages for years to come in David's life and in the lives of his family and in all Israel.[1]

THE SIN AND HOW IT HAPPENED (2 Sam. 11:1-27)

To this point in David's life he had been very actively and personally involved in warfare against the enemies of Israel. Under his leadership the Israelites had defeated nearly everyone that was a threat to their security. And at this juncture David was relatively free from military responsibility. He gladly turned over his direct leadership to Joab, his faithful military commander, who could easily handle any final skirmishes against their enemies. No one would deny that David had earned the right to relax and enjoy his position as king. He was now about 50 years old, having spent many of those years in active duty as a warrior on the front lines.

David and Bathsheba

One afternoon David was resting. He arose from his bed and went out on the roof of his house, a vantage point that gave him a bird's-eye view of most of Jerusalem. As he walked about viewing the city, he couldn't help noticing a beautiful woman bathing on a nearby rooftop. The Bible states that she was indeed *"very beautiful* in appearance" (11:2). Being a red-blooded man, David quickly responded to what he saw.

We're not sure of all the details leading up to the events recorded in the Bible, but some Bible scholars believe that Bathsheba may have purposely been trying to seduce David. This of course is feasible since she no doubt had noticed the king on many occasions strolling on his rooftop.

But even if this be true—and I think it probably was—what David did was inexcusable. He found out who she was, sent for her and committed adultery.

In David's mind the event was over. But not so! Bathsheba conceived and she sent word about it to David. Had David been just one of the pagan kings who ruled in the world at that time, he would have solved the problem quickly and easily. He would have simply taken Bathsheba into his household, not caring what happened to her husband or who knew about it. Or he could have ignored her plight. Since the king was considered sovereign by his people, he could do anything he wanted to. He was above the law since he made the laws. In most of the kingdoms there was no lawgiver superior to the kings themselves.

But David was no ordinary king. He'd been "anointed by God" and he served a Lawgiver far superior to himself, One who had thundered from Mount Sinai many years before: "You shall not commit *adultery* . . . . You shall not covet your neighbor's house; you shall not covet your neighbor's *wife* or his male servant or his female servant or his ox or his donkey or anything that belongs to your neighbor" (Exod. 20:14,17).

David had sinned against God. To this point in his life it was his greatest sin! But in his position as king of

Israel, as he had done on previous occasions, he did not immediately acknowledge his mistake. It appears he even refused to recognize it as a mistake. He attempted to solve the problem by himself, only getting himself in deeper.

David and Uriah

First, David tried the most logical thing he could think of. "I'll send for Uriah, Bathsheba's husband," he thought. "I'll make him believe that I've sent for him to find out the welfare of Joab and the state of war. Then I'll give him some time off to spend with his wife. He'll never know the child is mine" (see 2 Sam. 11:7).

Thus David reasoned and thus he acted! But ironically and to his surprise, his simple, logical scheme didn't work. His great wisdom that had defeated armies could not deliver him from this self-predicament. Uriah would not go home. In fact, he "slept at the door of the king's house with all the servants of his lord" (11:9). He was so loyal to David and to his fellow soldiers who were camping in the open battlefield, he would not allow himself the indulgence of staying in the comforts of his own home and enjoying the favors of his wife.

David's next scheme was to blur Uriah's thinking and to dull his selfless attitude. He purposely got Uriah drunk, hoping he would stumble on home and forget his military responsibilities, at least for one evening.

But again, David's strategy failed. Even in his drunken stupor, Uriah would not go home. He stayed in the king's court and slept in the servants' quarters.

By this time David was frustrated. What was he going to do? In the biblical account it appears he was both scared and angry—two emotions that frequently go together at times like this. And in his state of emotional turmoil, he made a decision that is incredible. He decided to have Uriah killed—"legitimately," that is—so it would appear he died in battle. Then David would be free, at least in the eyes of Israel, to take Bathsheba as one of his wives. Then no one except the cooperating parties would know.

This time David's scheme worked. He wrote a letter to Joab, sending it by Uriah himself, and instructed his military commander to send Bathsheba's husband to the front lines and under such conditions that he would not escape enemy fire. And when word came of his death, David brought Bathsheba "to his house and she became his wife" (11:27).

David and God

From a human point of view it appears that the problem was solved. And if David had been an ordinary king, life would have gone on as usual. But, again we must point out that David was no ordinary king. He was God's anointed. Consequently, "the thing that David had done was evil in the sight of the Lord" (11:27). Not only did he violate the law of God by committing adultery but, in his efforts to cover up his sin, he lied, he stole what did not belong to him and he committed murder. All of these acts violated the specific laws of God who had also thundered from Sinai: "You shall not *steal*. You shall not bear false witness *against your neighbor . . . . You shall not murder*" (Exod. 20:15,16,13).

DAVID'S SIN UNVEILED (2 Sam. 12:1-7)

For nearly a year David covered his sin, refusing to acknowledge it to himself, to the Lord and to the people of Israel. Then one day a strange thing happened. The Lord sent Nathan the prophet to see David. Nathan told the king a story:

> *There were two men in one city, the one rich and the other poor.*
> *The rich man had a great many flocks and herds.*

But the poor man had nothing except one little
   ewe lamb
Which he bought and nourished;
And it grew up together with him and his children.
It would eat of his bread and drink of his cup
   and lie in his bosom,
And was like a daughter to him.
Now a traveler came to the rich man,
And he was unwilling to take from his own flock
   or his own herd,
To prepare for the wayfarer who had come to him;
Rather he took the poor man's ewe lamb and
   prepared it for the man who had come to him.
(2 Sam. 12:1-4)

As David listened to Nathan's story, his anger was aroused against the man who had done such a selfish thing. His sense of justice rose within him and he interrupted Nathan's story with words of judgment: "As the Lord lives, surely the man who has done this deserves to die. And he must make restitution for the lamb fourfold, because he did this thing and had no compassion" (2 Sam. 12:5,6).

At this moment David was so self-deceived he did not understand he was pronouncing judgment on himself. He did not see *himself* in the story. But with his anger and his severe reaction he was projecting his own repressed guilt and anxiety. The extent of this projection is seen in his exaggerated response. The Law of Moses clearly stated that under these conditions a man only needed to give back four sheep for the one he had stolen (see Exod. 22:1). David's response was that a man like this "deserves to die."

David was speaking about himself and didn't realize it. God, who knows the depths of men's hearts, turned Nathan into a master psychologist, helping him to use a projective technique that has been unequaled in all of history.

At this moment Nathan moved from storytelling to interpretation. In the midst of David's emotional identification and reactions, he suddenly pulled David's mask from his blinded eyes so that he could see clearly his self-imposed deception. "You are the man!" said Nathan (2 Sam. 12:7).

Nathan's words were like a knife plunging into David's heart. His anger turned to grief and remorse. His fiery response turned to meekness. His world of greatness suddenly crumbled around him as he saw himself as he was—an adulterer, liar, thief, even a murderer! He was the man who deserved to die—not only on one count, but on several! In fact, David himself had sentenced men to death for lesser crimes against the laws of God!

THE RESULTS OF DAVID'S SINS (2 Sam. 12:8-23)

Though David clearly deserved the death penalty (see Lev. 20:10; 24:17), God forgave David because of his repentant and remorseful heart. Even in the Old Testament God's grace was evident in the life of His children. David's experience highlights that grace.

But God could not and would not eliminate the natural consequences of this sin. God's judgment was twofold. First, the child born to Bathsheba died, causing David unusual grief (see 2 Sam. 12:15-20). But the second result of his sin was long range. David's own household would be in a constant state of upheaval the rest of his life. And it happened just as God said it would (see 2 Sam. 12:10-12). One of his sons Amnon raped his sister Tamar. Absalom, another of David's sons, became so angry at Amnon for his horrible deed against their sister that he murdered Amnon (see 2 Sam. 13).

This was just the beginning of sorrows for David. In

time, Absalom rebelled against David and turned the hearts of the children of Israel against him. David had to flee for his life from Jerusalem with just a few faithful followers. Eventually, Absalom attacked David in battle planning to kill his own father (see 2 Sam. 14—18); however, in the process, Absalom lost his own life— adding sorrow upon sorrow to David (see 2 Sam. 18:15).

All of this resulted from David's sin. The sword never did depart from David's household, just as God had said (see 2 Sam. 12:10). Even his son, Solomon, who eventually replaced David as the king of Israel, followed in his father's footsteps and disobeyed God in many of the same areas David did.

SOME IMPORTANT OBSERVATIONS

David had experienced an unprecedented period of success both in his personal life and in his relationship with the children of Israel. Though David was certainly subject to the same routine mistakes all human beings make, for 20 years he had lived a godly life relatively free from serious mistakes such as he had made in the past. As king of Israel he had brought security and safety to his people. At no time in history had Israel demonstrated so well to the outside world their commitment to God and to each other. This dynamic in Israel was definitely a reflection of David's leadership.

It was following this significant period of success and his brilliant career as king of Israel—demonstrating wisdom, justice and righteousness—that David committed the most unwise, unjust and unrighteous act of his life.

David was idle with little to do but relax and enjoy his position as king. David had lived a very busy and active life. Never since his days as a shepherd boy had he so much leisure time. And while he was busy doing nothing he became vulnerable to Satan's attack. Rather than filling his thoughts with God and His greatness as he had done in his younger years, David allowed his mind to think about himself and his own needs.

The lesson for twentieth-century Christians comes through loud and clear. Beware of idleness and boredom. It is often the devil's workshop. This leads us to another observation.

David had developed a life-style where he could do almost anything he wanted to do and get anything he desired. David's central problem was not a cold uncaring wife who did not love him or meet his emotional and physical needs. If it had been, his behavior may have been more understandable but, of course, still inexcusable. David had wives and concubines galore, many of whom were ready and willing to spend an evening with King David. This was not his problem.

David's primary problem was that, combined with his sense of accomplishment and his idleness and boredom, he had a mind-set that he could really do almost anything and get away with it. After all he was king. Hadn't he unselfishly given himself to help Israel find security and direction in their life? Somehow, David must have rationalized that he had a right to spend an evening with Bathsheba.

This kind of rationalization happens easily to people who are in the habit of being successful. They want what they want when they want it. Suddenly they become a law unto themselves, throwing all moral values to the wind—even those they have most defended. Beware of rationalization under these circumstances.

David had violated God's law in multiplying wives and concubines. Polygamy poses somewhat of a problem to the twentieth-century Christian who is used to thinking in terms of God's standards in the New Testament.

138

What about this practice among Old Testament greats?

First, it must be stated that polygamy was never God's plan for men. Otherwise, He would have created more than one wife for Adam or more than one husband for Eve. His perfect will was that these two people find fellowship and fulfillment in each other.

When sin entered the world, however, it affected God's perfect plan for mankind in many ways, including the area of sexual relationship. Because of sin in the world man hardened his heart, and because of this hardening God tolerated polygamy, but He never willed it. And whenever it happened, there were always serious problems of jealousy, quarreling, crime and sensual indulgence. In fact, in the case of a king, God specifically forbade what David did. In the law which he revealed to Moses, he specifically warned that no future king of Israel should ever "multiply wives for himself, lest his heart turn away" (Deut. 17:17). This law David ignored.

More than any one thing, disobedience contributed to David's failure in this moment of his life. Related to this disobedience was the motive of pride. Pagan kings, being the only ones who normally could afford a large harem, took great pride in their female possessions. Evidently David fell prey to this worldly mentality and life-style in order to demonstrate his greatness in the world of kingship. Probably thinking he would draw the line in further disobedience, he found himself stepping over the line before he knew what happened.

David allowed temptation to turn into an act of sin. No one would fault David for responding emotionally to what he saw. Bathsheba was a beautiful woman. His initial passion and desire were not sin. His act of disobedience came when he lusted in his heart. That is, he deliberately sought her out for the purpose of having a sexual relationship.

David did not acknowledge his sin immediately and take action to correct it. Rather, he tried to cover up his act which led to another serious sin—murder. This was not a new development in David's life. Twenty years before, he faced the same dilemma in the land of the Philistines. One sin led to another when he tried to work it out by himself. Fortunately, God, in that situation through pure grace delivered David from his own connivings before his actions were irreversible.

David denied the reality of this sin and consequently deceived himself. Evidently the guilt and anxiety became so great for David that he eventually repressed his wrongdoing from his conscious thoughts. Thus when Nathan first approached him he saw no relationship between the story he heard and his own life.

David took advantage of God's grace once too often and suffered terrible consequences. When David was about to kill innocent shepherds because of Nabal's personal rejection, God stopped him through Abigail. Had he done what he had intended to do, it would have been a terrible blight on his reputation as a future king of Israel.

Again, when David was about to enter a battle with the Philistine army against Israel, God delivered him from a predicament he had created for himself. Again, God stopped him from a serious action which would have thwarted God's will for his life.

But there comes a time in a man's life when he must bear the responsibility for his own actions. When David decided to commit adultery with Bathsheba, God did not stand in his way. He had taken advantage of God's grace one time too often.

The consequences of David's sins were far greater than

they would have been for the average man on the street.
David was *the* spiritual and political leader in Israel. All
eyes were on him. He was known as "a man after God's
own heart." Consequently, the results of this sin were
far-reaching. Unfortunately, those most affected were
his own family members. But in this case the results
extended to all Israel. He lost respect with his own
people and even among the pagans of the land.

*Though David and many of his loved ones and all of
Israel suffered the consequences of his sin, God forgave
David personally because of his sincere confession and
contrite heart.* David's prayer for forgiveness is recorded in Psalm 51:

> *Be gracious to me, O God, according to Thy
>   lovingkindness;*
> *According to the greatness of Thy compassion
>   blot out my transgressions.*
> *Wash me thoroughly from my iniquity,*
> *And cleanse me from my sin.*
> *For I know my transgressions,*
> *And my sin is ever before me.*
> *Against Thee, Thee only, I have sinned,*
> *And done what is evil in Thy sight,*
> *So that Thou art justified when Thou dost speak,*
> *And blameless when Thou dost judge.*
> . . . .
> *Purify me with hyssop, and I shall be clean;*
> *Wash me; and I shall be whiter than snow.*
> *Make me to hear joy and gladness,*
> *Let the bones which Thou hast broken rejoice.*
> *Hide Thy face from my sins,*
> *And blot out all my iniquities.*
> *Create in me a clean heart, O God,*
> *And renew a steadfast spirit within me.*
> (Ps. 51:1-4; 7-12)

The answer to David's prayer is recorded in Psalm 32:

> *How blessed is he whose transgression is forgiven,*
> *Whose sin is covered!*
> *How blessed is the man to whom the Lord does not*
>   *impute iniquity,*
> *And in whose spirit there is no deceit!*
>
> *When I kept silent about my sin,*
>   *my body wasted away*
> *Through my groaning all day long.*
> *For day and night Thy hand was heavy upon me;*
> *My vitality was drained away as with the fever-*
>   *heat of summer.*
> *I acknowledged my sin to Thee,*
> *And my iniquity I did not hide;*
> *I said, "I will confess my transgressions*
>   *to the Lord";*
> *And Thou didst forgive the guilt of my sin.*
> (Ps. 32:1-5)

TWENTIETH-CENTURY LESSONS

These observations regarding David's failure surface some very obvious lessons for twentieth-century Christians.

No Christian should rely on past success as security from failure in the future. At any moment, at any hour, any Christian anywhere can be caught off guard and fail God miserably. Fortunately, most of our failures are not as serious as David's, but they can be. This is particularly true of Christians who are well-known for their dynamic leadership. And moral failure is usually the culprit. I've seen this happen to men in the ministry and what a heyday Satan has had. The results are devastating to the man's family and to the Body of Christ. The failure becomes a tragic stumbling block to the unsaved world. The story of David has written across it in flashing red lights the words of Paul, "If you think you are standing firm, be careful that you don't fall!" (1 Cor. 10:12).

Beware of idleness and boredom. It is often the devil's workshop. Many a Christian has fallen prey to Satan when he has been busy doing nothing.

Note: This does not mean Christians should not have periods of relaxation and vacation.

The kind of rationalization that David engaged in happens easily to people who are in the habit of being successful. They want what they want when they want it. Suddenly they become a law unto themselves and sometimes throw all moral values to the wind, even those they have most defended.

Beware of developing a sensuous life-style. Though you may not be a polygamist in the strict sense of that word, multiple sexual experiences with a variety of people will make any person doubly vulnerable to Satan's attacks in this area of his life. People living in the twentieth century and in our present decade are particularly vulnerable to developing this life-style. If you are a new Christian coming out of this background, beware! Satan is standing ready to trip you up at the slightest provocation.

Beware that temptation does not turn into sin. Any desire in one's heart is only one step away from the act. Remember also that Jesus classified intent to sin as wrong as the act itself. This is what He meant when He said, "But I tell you that anyone who looks at a woman lustfully has already committed adultery with her in his heart" (Matt. 5:28).

Note: Temptation is not lust. If it were, most men living in the twentieth century would commit adultery every day of their lives. Lust is that process whereby an individual decides to commit sin through an improper act.

Do not try to cover up or hide sin. Very frequently it will lead to an even more serious sin.

Acknowledge sin immediately—especially to God. Handle guilt and anxiety through confession. Don't repress these feelings. If you do, it will eventually lead to self-deception, a hardened heart, and a seared conscience.

Do not take advantage of God's grace. Remember, the Bible says that there comes a time when "God gives man up" to do what he wants to do.

Remember that the greater our responsibility the greater our accountability. The higher our position the greater we fall. The more people who are involved in our lives, the more there are who are hurt through our failures.

No matter what your sin and its consequences, confess it and do what is right. Accept God's forgiveness in Jesus Christ. At this point, follow David's example. After he confessed his sin and received forgiveness, he accepted the consequences of his sin. Then he "arose from the ground, washed, anointed himself, and changed his clothes; and he came into the house of the Lord and worshiped" (2 Sam. 12:20).

A PERSONAL PROJECT
Evaluate your own life-style in the light of the lessons

we can learn from David's experience. Remember, these lessons apply to all of God's commandments such as idolatry, taking His name in vain, honoring father and mother, stealing, bearing false witness, coveting, etc., in addition to illicit sex.

Isolate your own areas of vulnerability and ask God to help you by His Holy Spirit to be obedient to His Word. Remember Paul's words to the Romans: "Therefore, there is now no condemnation for those who are in Christ Jesus, because through Christ Jesus the law of the Spirit of life set me free from the law of sin and death. For what the law was powerless to do in that it was weakened by our sinful nature, God did by sending his own Son in the likeness of sinful man to be a sin offering. And so he condemned sin in sinful man, in order that the righteous requirements of the law might be fully met in us, who do not live according to our sinful nature but according to the Spirit" (Rom. 8:1-4).

Note

1. David was 30 years old when he became king of Judah. He reigned seven and one-half years in Judah and 33 years over all Israel. His total reign lasted approximately 40 years (see 2 Sam. 5:4,5).

13

DAVID'S LIFE IN PERSPECTIVE

1 Samuel 16:1—2 Samuel 24:25

Looking at each major event in David's life has surfaced some dynamic lessons—lessons that can help us be more dynamic Christians living in the twentieth-century world. But in order not to miss some of the richest lessons from David's life, it is imperative that we look back over his life and gain an overall perspective. In fact, we can only discern these overarching lessons as we observe the specific events as they unfold over a period of years and as they are observed in relationship to each other. In other words David's life, like any person's life, was not a series of isolated experiences. Rather, the very ebb and flow, the ups and downs in his life from the time he was anointed by Samuel until the day he died provide every Christian living today with valuable spiritual insights and lessons. Why did David experience high points and low points in his journey through life?

OBSERVATION NUMBER ONE

God anointed David as king of Israel on the basis of his heart attitude at the time of his anointing.

In some respects this is an observation that is difficult to comprehend. God is omniscient and sovereign. He knows the end from the beginning and every detail in between. He is in control of the universe. His perspective is eternal. And yet He instructed Samuel to anoint David on the basis of his spiritual condition as a young shepherd who loved and honored his heavenly Father. When Saul chose to disobey God, it was in the process of space and time that the Lord "sought out for Himself a man after His own heart" (1 Sam. 13:14). And David was that man. Because of this young shepherd's view of God's attributes (His omnipotence, His omniscience, His omnipresence, His loving concern, His faithfulness, His righteousness and His holiness) and because of David's own heart which was characterized by faith, thankfulness, honesty, openness, expectancy, humility, dependence, and repentance—because of these qualities —God instructed Samuel to anoint him as the future king of Israel, to eventually replace Saul.

It's abundantly clear, however, from David's total life story that he was not always this kind of man. There were periods of time when he ceased being a "man after God's own heart." At times he woefully failed God, did his own thing, walked directly and deliberately out of the will of God, and indulged in some incredible sins.

The Lord knew, of course, that David would fail Him in these areas of his life before He even chose him. But it was not within God's predetermined plan that David fail. In some remarkable way, the sovereign God of the universe anointed David to be king of Israel based upon his spiritual successes in the here and now, not upon his future failures.

How can this be? From a human perspective there is

147

no satisfactory explanation except that God is God and He did it and can do it without violating His omniscience and His providence. And the fact is that David could have been a "man after God's own heart" *all* of his life and on a consistent basis if he had obeyed God and lived by the same spiritual guidelines he followed as a young dedicated Hebrew.

The same opportunity lay before King Saul who was anointed by God and promised continual blessing, in fact eternal blessings, if he only walked in the Lord's ways (see 1 Sam. 12:14). Like David, Saul's failure was not predetermined. In fact, God was terribly distressed when Saul disobeyed Him. Twice we read in 1 Samuel 15 that "The Lord *regretted* that He had made Saul king over Israel" (1 Sam. 15:35; see also v. 11).

Again, how can this be? How can a sovereign God regret His own decisions when He knows the end from the beginning? We must conclude that there is no satisfactory human explanation. It is beyond our finite minds. And if you tried to explain this concept totally you would end up with an extreme theological position that ignores certain realities in Scripture. The fact is that in some remarkable and incomprehensible way, God honors man's freedom and makes His decisions accordingly. And part of that decision-making process involves dealing with us at any given period of time in our life. Because David was indeed a man after God's heart, He anointed him to replace the man who had woefully failed Him. Had Saul not failed, had he obeyed the Lord, God would have dealt with him according to His promise and all the factors would have fallen naturally into place, including David's role in His sovereign plan.

What about you? God also deals with us on the basis of our present heart attitudes. The fact that we have warm sensitive hearts toward God *now* is no guarantee

148

that we will be that kind of person 10, 20, or 30 years from now. And the fact that God is using us *now* to achieve His purposes because of our spiritual life-style and commitment to Him is no guarantee He will use us in the future. If we, like David, eventually ignore God's will we too will have to pay the natural consequences.

Unfortunately, I've seen this thing happen to one of my closest friends, a man who was indeed sensitive toward God and people. He was one of the best Bible teachers I've ever known. He graduated from seminary with the highest honors, earning a doctorate in theology. Many people's lives were changed because of his ministry. But little by little he turned aside from obeying the Word of God. Today he is divorced from his wife and separated from his family; he is out of the Christian ministry and continuing to live out of God's will. Hopefully, like David, he'll one day come to his senses and once again become a man after God's heart. And if he does, God will forgive him and restore him, though he will certainly have to face the natural consequences of his sin.

The lesson is clear for each one of us. What we are *now*, and how God is using us *now* certainly is no guarantee for the future. It depends on our continual commitment to the Lord and our constant obedience.

OBSERVATION NUMBER TWO

David's failures were always related to the fact that he failed to consult God regarding His will; conversely, his restoration was always correlated with renewed communication with God.

One of the primary reasons David was a man after God's heart rests in the fact that he communicated with God. He spent many hours in personal communion with his heavenly Father. And David had a great capacity for hearing and "seeing" God in what He created—upon the waters, in the wind, through the lightning and the thunder, in the rain showers, upon the green meadows and in the valleys, and as the golden grain was harvested (see Pss. 29; 65).

David was also one of those Old Testament saints who experienced reciprocal communication with God. He often sought God's will about certain decisions and received a direct answer from the Lord. However, in each instance where he walked out of God's will there is no evidence that he consulted God about the matter. In fact, he even ignored the truth that God had already revealed.

But by contrast, it is also true that each time David refocused his spiritual life he once again consulted the Lord. This was true following the tremendous bout with fear which led him to scheme and lie in order to escape from Saul (see 1 Sam. 21). And once he came to his senses, his first action was to seek God's will through prayer (see 1 Sam. 23:4,10-12). And the Lord in His love and grace answered him and gave him specific directions.

This pattern is also evident when David lost complete perspective and sought asylum in the land of the Philistines. David did not consult the Lord at all. He made his own decision based upon his own human reactions. And this time he managed to get into even deeper trouble.

But as before, he eventually regained perspective. When he did, one of his first actions involved prayer. After what appears to be more than a year with no direct communication with the Lord and of acting purely out of human engineering, David once again "strengthened himself in the Lord his God" (1 Sam. 30:6). It was then that he found himself back on the straight and narrow path, doing what God wanted him to do.

What about you? Once again the lesson is clear! If we

150

are to *remain in God's* will throughout our life we must *seek* God's will. We must consult the Lord.

Today God has not chosen to speak to His children by direct revelation as He did with certain Old and New Testament saints, men like Abraham, Moses, David, Peter, John and especially Paul. But God has spoken to all of us through His Word, the Bible. We have at our disposal His direct revelation in written form. The Scriptures contain all we need to discover His perfect will throughout our lifetime. The question is: Are we consulting His Word regularly in order to discover His will? And do we take advantage of the opportunity to consult Him directly through prayer as Paul has exhorted us to do? (see Phil. 4:6).

Most Christians I know who are in serious trouble today are people who are trying to scheme and engineer their way through mountains of difficulty without consulting God's will through His Word and prayer. In fact, I once knew a Christian who wandered around in the land of the Philistines trying to impress the world. He was out of the will of God. Consequently he got in trouble with the government, his business associates, his family and his Christian friends. As long as he ignored God's will he went from bad to worse, just like David! What about you?

OBSERVATION NUMBER THREE

Closely related to David's failure to consult God regarding His will was his tendency to stop trusting God and to take matters into his own hands.

When David challenged Goliath he did so with great confidence in God to deliver this huge Philistine into his hands (see 1 Sam. 17:45). And God did. But when his faith turned into fear he immediately began to scheme and connive so that he utterly failed to do God's will. But when his fear turned back to faith, David once again became successful. He was able to balance his human skills with the dependence upon God to use those skills to achieve His divine purposes. This is very clear in David's life when he emerged from the cave of Adullam and faced both the Philistine army as well as King Saul (see 1 Sam. 23). It is also true when he came to his senses in the land of the Philistines and once again trusted God (see 1 Sam. 30).

What about you? How easy it is for a Christian to trust in himself, to take matters into his own hands when he faces a serious problem. I find that this is one of my own greatest tendencies. And when I do, very seldom do things work out as they should. Though careful planning and human effort are essential in solving problems, they must be carefully balanced with trust and confidence in the Lord. There must be a proper integration between human and divine factors.

OBSERVATION NUMBER FOUR
David's greatest failures always followed a period of great success and popularity.

There were three such cycles in David's life. The *first* began with his great victory over Goliath, leading to unparalleled popularity. The theme song in Israel was that "Saul has slain his thousands, and David his ten thousands" (1 Sam. 18:7). For a period of time all David did turned out right. He "was prospering in all his ways for the Lord was with him" (1 Sam. 18:14). But all of this ended with a period of great failure as David attempted to escape Saul's attacks on his life with his own schemes.

The *second* period of success involved his unusual graciousness toward Saul when he had two unique opportunities to take the king's life. With all patience and nobleness he rose above the temptation and demonstrated great love for his enemy. Though his testimony was limited to his own band of men, he had experienced an unusual spiritual victory. But again this mountain peak experience resulted in a period of great failure, as he traveled into the land of the Philistines seeking refuge.

The *third* period of success was the longest in his life, approximately 20 years. Though not without mistakes, David lived a well-ordered and God-fearing life. As the king of Israel he ruled his people with wisdom and righteousness. His popularity was not only prevalent among his own people but also among most of the nations that surrounded Israel. And it was at this time that he committed his greatest sins—adultery and murder—which introduced a period of stress and anxiety that plagued him the rest of his life. Though he experienced forgiveness from God, trouble knocked at his door until the day he died.

What about you? Perhaps this is one of the greatest lessons we can learn from the overall events in David's life. We must be on constant guard during a period of great success and popularity in our lives. It is during these periods that Satan can attack us on our blind side. How easy it is to be lifted up with pride and take credit and glory for ourselves. And when we do, we are candidates for failure. We are tempted to stop consulting God. We are tempted to take matters into our own hands. We are tempted to stop trusting God and to have faith only in ourselves.

OBSERVATION NUMBER FIVE

David misinterpreted his success and popularity as a sign of God's blanket approval on all he was doing.

This observation is closely related to the previous one. But it is worthy of special consideration. This was one of David's greatest mistakes.

His sojourn into the land of the Philistines is the classic illustration of this fallacious thinking. Though he was living directly out of God's will in many ways, he still prospered. How easy it was to misinterpret and misconstrue these events as God's blessing.

But after David became king of all Israel, he "became greater and greater, for the Lord God of hosts was with him" (2 Sam. 5:10). This verse of Scripture is almost haunting in its implications.

Here David's greatness is measured by his success as king, his popularity with the people of Israel and his victories over his enemies. And it was indeed a blessing from God. But David did not realize that rising to popularity and success in this life is not necessarily a measurement of spiritual maturity, even though God may be adding the blessing. In fact, part of David's greatness in the eyes of the world was the number of concubines and wives he added to his harem—a direct violation of God's commands (see 2 Sam. 5:13; Deut. 17:17). An overview on the events in David's life clearly reveals a man who was experiencing unprecedented greatness in the eyes of men as a direct blessing from God, but at the same time experiencing a deterioration in his spiritual sensitivities which had so much characterized his inner being as a young man in love with his Creator. From the time he left his father's flocks to his great victory over Goliath, David reached his spiritual peak. And from that time forward, he experienced ups and downs. But it appears it was never on as high a level as in his early years.

What about you? Is this kind of spiritual experience inevitable, especially as we get older? Not at all! David's life could have been a series of mountaintop experiences with the Lord. Obviously, he would need to pass through various valleys to climb to higher levels but he did not *have* to slide off the other side of the mountain.

Here is a great lesson for every twentieth-century Christian. Many of us tend to interpret success and popularity as God's blanket approval on all we are doing. Not so! God's grace is poured out on *all* men. And, no matter what our relationship with Him, He often continues to bless us materially and socially. And if we're not careful, our spiritual life in the eyes of the Lord can be deteriorating while our "greatness" in the eyes of men can be increasing.

How tragic for David! And how tragic when this happens to a Christian. In some instances it also leads to a catastrophe—a Bathsheba, dishonesty, a broken family, children who turn against God.

There are Christian leaders (and Christians generally) who, in the eyes of others, are climbing the ladder of success and popularity. But in their hearts they have lost the warmth toward God and people they once knew when they first began their ministry. With popularity has come professionalism, spiritual pride and a spirit of competition. In some instances these people eventually passed off the scene and are living fruitless and carnal lives. They lose credibility with their own family members.

OBSERVATION NUMBER SIX

David's greatest sin, adultery and murder, in many respects disqualified him from correcting and disciplining his own children when they committed the same sins.

What could David say when his son Amnon raped his own sister Tamar? And what right did he have to deal with his son Absalom when he in turn murdered Amnon for raping his sister?

Obviously, he still had the responsibility to discipline his children even though he had committed sins just as flagrant as they. But how could he? Emotionally he was thwarted. The finger of ridicule and condemnation would be pointed at him from all directions. "What right have you to deal with us for our sins when you, the king of Israel—a 'man of God'—have committed the same crimes?"

David never overcame this problem. His loss of respect was too great. The emotional damage in his own heart was too deep to be healed completely. Forgiven? Yes! Totally exonerated in the eyes of the people? No! He bore the stigma of this failure until his death.

What about you? There are Christian people today who, like David, have emotionally and socially disqualified themselves from disciplining their own children. They have destroyed their credibility. Their words of admonition have a hollow ring. "Do what I say and not what I do" is their only recourse. And the response either in muffled words or in flagrant rebellion is always the same: "Hypocrite! What right have you to tell me what I can or cannot do, what is best for me, when you are as guilty as I am!"

Fortunately, most of us have not blown it nearly so badly as David. And in most instances children are very understanding and forgiving when they see true repentance on our part. But there is a point beyond which we cannot go without serious repercussions. David passed that point, in a sense the point of no return, when it came to regaining respect from his own children.

Again, how tragic! And how on guard we must be that it not happen to us as Christian parents living in the twentieth century! And it need not happen. For the great majority of Christians there is a very bright future. And how great is our advantage to have recorded for us the example of David, who made such a great beginning but, in many respects, ended his life with a dark cloud over what could have been a consistently brilliant and exemplary career and walk with God. All of these things are recorded for us that we might avoid his mistakes. The question is: How willing am I to listen and to learn?

OBSERVATION NUMBER SEVEN

Each time David acknowledged his sin and truly repented, God forgave and restored him to fellowship with Himself.

Though David on several occasions walked out of God's will, there came a point in his life when he always turned back to the Lord with great remorse and sorrow, seeking God's forgiveness. In many respects this is why he was called a man after God's own heart. Though he at times certainly could not be characterized as this kind of man, the fact remains that he always had a sensitive and responsive heart toward God which caused him to respond in repentance. Thus, his gravestone could legitimately have carried this epitaph: "Here lies David, a man after God's heart (often but not always)!"

What about you? In the New Testament David is most frequently mentioned in conjunction with the lineage of Jesus Christ. Our Lord and Saviour is often called the Son of David. In fact, His direct line can be traced from David's offspring through Bathsheba! (see Matt. 1:6). And if this is surprising, if you trace Christ's lineage back further, Jesus' great ... great ... grandmother was Rahab the harlot, who was converted to the God of Israel out of the pagan city of Jericho (Matt. 1:5).

What does all of this mean? Perhaps most significantly it means that Jesus Christ not only identified with our failures in His life on earth ("We have one who has been tempted in every way, just as we are—yet was without sin" Heb. 4:15), but He also identified with the greatest failures of mankind in His heritage. His purity and His sinless life were not dependent upon His ancestry. It could not have been, "For all have sinned and fall short of the glory of God" (Rom. 3:23).

But at the human level—something we will spend eternity attempting to understand—Jesus Christ identified with our sins without sinning. And because He did, He understands our temptations. He is our great high priest who is able to "sympathize with our weaknesses" (Heb. 4:15). Were He not this kind of Saviour no man could be saved—including His great . . . great . . . grandfather, David.

Have you accepted Jesus Christ as your Saviour from sin? Have you confessed your sins and experienced the cleansing power of His shed blood? If not, do so today. Simply in your own words invite Him to be your Saviour.

And as a Christian, perhaps you are living out of God's will. Like David, you have blown it. Then, like David, acknowledge your sin, repent and turn back to God. Remember that "if we confess our sins, he is faithful and just and will forgive us our sins and purify us from all unrighteousness" (1 John 1:9). If God's mercy was available to a repentant heart in the Old Testament, and it was, as David's life dramatically demonstrates, how much then is His mercy available in the New Testament! Turn back to God now before it's too late to experience the earthly benefits of that forgiveness.

A PERSONAL PROJECT

1. To what extent am I assuming that my present heart attitude toward God (also assuming it is warm and responsive) will continue throughout my lifetime?

2. To what extent do I consult God through His Word and in prayer in the course of setting up my life goals?

3. To what extent in living my daily life do I tend to

stop trusting God and to take matters into my own hands?

4. To what extent am I on guard against spiritual pride and an overconfident attitude when I am experiencing a period of great success in my life?

5. To what extent do I interpret my successes in life and my popularity as a sign of God's approval on all that I am doing?

6. To what extent am I allowing attitudes and actions to creep into my life that will eventually cause me to lose credibility with those I love the most?

7. To what extent am I availing myself of the resources in Jesus Christ to forgive my sins and then to turn from those sins. NOTE: It is possible to think about these guidelines too much, to actually be neurotic in our Christian life, constantly fearful we are going to make serious mistakes. God never intended for us to live this way. On the other hand, it is His will that we think about these guidelines sufficiently to avoid the same mistakes David made.

A FINAL WORD

If you are a young person with a lifetime before you, or if you're an older Christian who has walked with God since being a Christian, remember we need not follow in David's footsteps when it comes to his failures. The Bible says that "no temptation has seized you except what is common to man. And God is faithful; he will not let you be tempted beyond what you can bear. But when you are tempted, he will also provide a way out so that you can stand up under it" (1 Cor. 10:13). Learn from David's experience!